File for Divorce in Illinois

Fourth Edition

Diana Brodman Summers

Attorney at Law

SPHINX® PUBLISHING
AN IMPRINT OF SOURCEBOOKS, INC.®
NAPERVILLE, ILLINOIS
www.SphinxLegal.com

Fourth Edition: 2006

Published by: **Sphinx® Publishing, An Imprint of Sourcebooks, Inc.®**

<u>Naperville Office</u>
P.O. Box 4410
Naperville, Illinois 60567-4410
630-961-3900
Fax: 630-961-2168
www.sourcebooks.com
www.SphinxLegal.com

This publication is designed to provide accurate and authoritative information in regard to the subject matter covered. It is sold with the understanding that the publisher is not engaged in rendering legal, accounting, or other professional service. If legal advice or other expert assistance is required, the services of a competent professional person should be sought.

From a Declaration of Principles Jointly Adopted by a Committee of the American Bar Association and a Committee of Publishers and Associations

This product is not a substitute for legal advice.

Disclaimer required by Texas statutes.

Library of Congress Cataloging-in-Publication Data

Summers, Diana Brodman.
  File for divorce in Illinois / by Diana Brodman Summers.-- 4th ed.
      p. cm.
  Rev. ed. of: How to file for divorce in Illinois. 3rd ed. 2002.
  Includes index.
  ISBN-10 1-57248-510-8 (pbk. : alk. paper)
  ISBN-13 978-1-57248-510-5
  1. Divorce suits--Illinois--Popular works. 2. Divorce--Law and legislation--Illinois--Popular works. I. Summers, Diana Brodman. How to file for divorce in Illinois. II. Title.
  KFI1300.Z9S45 2006
  346.77301'66--dc22
                                                                    2006014837

Printed and bound in the United States of America.
BG — 10 9 8 7 6 5 4 3 2 1

Contents

Using Self-Help Law Books

Before using a self-help law book, you should realize the advantages and disadvantages of doing your own legal work and understand the challenges and diligence that this requires.

The Growing Trend

Rest assured that you will not be the first or only person handling your own legal matter. For example, in some states, more than 75% of the people in divorces and other cases represent themselves. Because of the high cost of legal services, this is a major trend, and many courts are struggling to make it easier for people to represent themselves. However, some courts are not happy with people who do not use attorneys and refuse to help them in any way. For some, the attitude is, "Go to the law library and figure it out for yourself."

We write and publish self-help law books to give people an alternative to the often complicated and confusing legal books found in most law libraries. We have made the explanations of the law as simple and easy to understand as possible. Of course, unlike an attorney advising an individual client, we cannot cover every conceivable possibility.

Cost/Value Analysis Whenever you shop for a product or service, you are faced with various levels of quality and price. In deciding what product or service to buy, you make a cost/value analysis on the basis of your willingness to pay and the quality you desire.

When buying a car, you decide whether you want transportation, comfort, status, or sex appeal. Accordingly, you decide among choices such as a Neon, a Lincoln, a Rolls Royce, or a Porsche. Before making a decision, you usually weigh the merits of each option against the cost.

When you get a headache, you can take a pain reliever (such as aspirin) or visit a medical specialist for a neurological examination. Given this choice, most people, of course, take a pain reliever, since it costs only pennies; whereas a medical examination costs hundreds of dollars and takes a lot of time. This is usually a logical choice because it is rare to need anything more than a pain reliever for a headache. But in some cases, a headache may indicate a brain tumor, and failing to see a specialist right away can result in complications. Should everyone with a headache go to a specialist? Of course not, but people treating their own illnesses must realize that they are betting on the basis of their cost/value analysis of the situation. They are taking the most logical option.

The same cost/value analysis must be made when deciding to do one's own legal work. Many legal situations are very straightforward, requiring a simple form and no complicated analysis. Anyone with a little intelligence and a book of instructions can handle the matter without outside help.

But there is always the chance that complications are involved that only an attorney would notice. To simplify the law into a book like this, several legal cases often must be condensed into a single sentence or paragraph. Otherwise, the book would be several hundred pages long and too complicated for most people. However, this simplification necessarily leaves out many details and nuances that would apply to special or unusual situations. Also, there are many ways to interpret most legal questions. Your case may come before a judge who disagrees with the analysis of our authors.

Therefore, in deciding to use a self-help law book and to do your own legal work, you must realize that you are making a cost/value analysis. You have decided that the money you will save in doing it yourself outweighs the chance that your case will not turn out to your satisfaction. Most people handling their own simple legal matters never have a problem, but occasionally people find that it ended up costing them more to have an attorney straighten out the situation than it would have if they had hired an attorney in the beginning. Keep this in mind while handling your case, and be sure to consult an attorney if you feel you might need further guidance.

Local Rules   The next thing to remember is that a book which covers the law for the entire nation, or even for an entire state, cannot possibly include every procedural difference of every jurisdiction. Whenever possible, we provide the exact form needed; however, in some areas, each county, or even each judge, may require unique forms and procedures. In our state books, our forms usually cover the majority of counties in the state or provide examples of the type of form that will be required. In our national books, our forms are sometimes even more general in nature but are designed to give a good idea of the type of form that will be needed in most locations. Nonetheless, keep in mind that your state, county, or judge may have a requirement, or use a form, that is not included in this book.

You should not necessarily expect to be able to get all of the information and resources you need solely from within the pages of this book. This book will serve as your guide, giving you specific information whenever possible and helping you to find out what else you will need to know. This is just like if you decided to build your own backyard deck. You might purchase a book on how to build decks. However, such a book would not include the building codes and permit requirements of every city, town, county, and township in the nation; nor would it include the lumber, nails, saws, hammers, and other materials and tools you would need to actually build the deck. You would use the book as your guide, and then do some work and research involving such matters as whether you need a permit of some kind, what type and grade of wood is available in your area, whether to use hand tools or power tools, and how to use those tools.

Before using the forms in a book like this, you should check with your court clerk to see if there are any local rules of which you should be aware or local forms you will need to use. Often, such forms will require the same information as the forms in the book but are merely laid out differently or use slightly different language. They will sometimes require additional information.

Changes in the Law   Besides being subject to local rules and practices, the law is subject to change at any time. The courts and the legislatures of all fifty states are constantly revising the laws. It is possible that while you are reading this book, some aspect of the law is being changed.

In most cases, the change will be of minimal significance. A form will be redesigned, additional information will be required, or a waiting period will be extended. As a result, you might need to revise a form, file an extra form, or wait out a longer time period. These types of changes will not usually affect the outcome of your case. On the other hand, sometimes a major part of the law is changed, the entire law in a particular area is rewritten, or a case that was the basis of a central legal point is overruled. In such instances, your entire ability to pursue your case may be impaired.

Introduction

The decision to end a marriage is extremely serious and will impact every aspect of your life, from financial health to physical health. Like marriage, a divorce should not be undertaken in haste or anger, especially if there are children involved. Before making such a life-altering decision, learn as much as you can about the process of divorcing, the financial ramifications of a divorce, the emotional toll, and the requirements of the law. This knowledge will prepare you for the certain ups and downs of a divorce.

A divorce is one of the most common and most traumatic encounters a person can have with the legal system. It can also be one of the most expensive events that needs to be paid for at a time when a person is least likely to have any extra funds. This book helps you obtain knowledge of the legal side of divorce and what to expect when getting a divorce in Illinois. If you decide to hire an attorney, this book assists you in working with your attorney in the most efficient manner, so that you will not be spending money in unnecessary legal fees.

This is not a law school course, but a consumer's guide to help you through the system. In many of the sections you will see actual Illinois law cited. This is a starting point for those who want to do their own legal research.

Even if all you are doing is *considering* getting a divorce, read this book before you make the first step, especially if children are involved. You should familiarize yourself with what to expect during a divorce so that you can be strong for yourself and your family during this stressful time.

Marriage and Divorce in Illinois

Years (or months) ago you made that very serious decision to spend the rest of your life *happily ever after* with that one special person as husband and wife. Now, perhaps that happily ever after has become a bad dream, and you are considering divorce. This chapter provides an explanation of the basics of marriage and divorce under Illinois law, information on the process of divorce, and things you will need to know to prepare yourself for the tough time ahead.

MARRIAGE

It sounds so simple, but you cannot get a divorce unless you are legally married. There are legal restrictions on entering into a marriage. To the extent the legal restrictions were followed determines whether you file for an annulment, a divorce, or if you can just sever the relationship without any legal procedure.

Marriage is a legal contract between a man and a woman, together with certain legal restrictions as directed by the state. It does not require a religious component. Each state has its own laws and restrictions on marriage. These individual restrictions are recognized by every other state. That means that if a couple was legally married in Nevada, they are considered married in Illinois (and every other state of the Union).

The most common misconception is with the term *common law marriage*, which is when two people live together for a period of time as husband and wife. Illinois does not recognize a common law marriage, regardless of the length of time that a couple lived together or the number of children born of that union. Those who never went through the legalities to become husband and wife can merely walk away from each other without the need of divorce or annulment. However, if there are minor children of this union, a court may require child support.

Illinois marriage laws are in Illinois Compiled Statutes (ILCS), Chapter 750, Sections (§§) 5/202 through 219. For a couple to be married under Illinois law, they must obtain a valid marriage license from the county where they intend to marry. A marriage license requires information on residency, age, prior marriages or divorces, and a health certificate from a doctor who performs a state-required blood test of communicative diseases. A marriage license will *not* be issued if:

- either party is 16 or 17 years old and does not have permission from the parent or guardian (see Chapter 2 on Annulments);

- either party is under 16 years old, even with permission of the parent or guardian;

- either party is still married to someone else;

- the couple is parent and child, brother and sister, uncle and niece, or aunt and nephew;

- the couple is first cousins to each other; or,

- both parties are the same sex.

Once a marriage license is issued, then a judge or religious official will assist the couple in pronouncing their vows. At that point, the couple and the judge or officiant sign the marriage certificate.

If you followed all the restrictions, then you are married and will need to file for a divorce. If one of the parties lacks the physical ability for sexual intercourse or has been legally declared mentally incapacitated, you may qualify for an *annulment*. (See Chapter 2 on Annulments.)

If you are not legally married but had children together, you still may be entitled to financial support for those minor children. If you are in that situation, you should probably seek assistance from an attorney who concentrates on child support issues.

DIVORCE

Divorce is the most common way to terminate the legal contract of marriage. Illinois calls divorce *dissolution of marriage*. Legally, a divorce:

- ✪ gives each party the right to marry someone else;

- ✪ divides the property and debts of the parties; and,

- ✪ determines the care and custody of the children of the marriage.

Divorce can be granted for several reasons, many of which place blame on one of the parties. Another reason is a no-fault ground called the *irretrievable breakdown of the marriage*. There are restrictions and requirements that come with each of these grounds. (See Chapter 6 on Divorce Basics.)

Many counties not only allow—but encourage—certain parties to file their own simplified divorce. This is usually restricted to those who have been married eight years or less, do not have children, do not have real estate, and meet some other requirements. See Chapter 7 on the Divorce Process for more information on this. Also, see Chapter 8 on Divorce Forms.

Alternatives to Divorce

While there are very few alternatives to divorcing that will work in this world, you may decide after reading this book that divorce is just too much work and expense to bother with. If you and your spouse feel that there is even the slightest chance to save the marriage, go for it. Many professional marriage counselors are available to help people who are thinking of divorcing. A marriage counselor may help you and your spouse back together, or may just give you the push that is needed to divorce.

You may consider a legal separation, where the spouses live apart and are bound by a legal settlement agreement. See Chapter 2 for information on legal separations and Chapter 11 for information on settlement agreements.

PSYCHOLOGICAL AND SOCIAL ISSUES OF DIVORCE

While this book concentrates on the legal issues of a divorce, the larger, more demanding issues are the psychological, emotional, and social ones. A divorce is one of the top stressful events in a person's life, right after death of a child, death of spouse, and death of parents. A divorce is also *a death* and those who go through a divorce should expect to go through the same stages of grief as they do when a family member dies.

No matter if you are the one who wanted the divorce or if your spouse did, you will grieve for what was lost. You have lost the companionship of that spouse, the social standing of being a couple, the finances of your spouse, and the security of knowing that there was someone who cared for you. Give yourself time to grieve and to cry for a dead relationship.

It is common for the person who initiated the divorce to have second thoughts because of the grief involved. Those who do not expect this feeling may misconstrue it as an indication that divorcing is not the right thing to do. Your spouse may start looking very good; all of his or her faults may suddenly go away. You may even go so far as to think about having sexual relations with this person as a way to dull the pain of the grief. Remember that this feeling of grief is normal and everyone who divorces feels this to some extent. Grief is not a sign of anything other than the fact that you are leaving a known way of living for an unknown. It will be scary, as most major changes are.

Talking about Marital Problems

When people have marital problems, they sometimes crave talking about them to friends and family. It is a way to validate their side of arguments, to get some sympathy, or to feel that they are right. However, talking to friends and family will not solve the problems between you and your spouse; it only allows others into a private situation. A good rule of thumb begins long before you file for divorce—do not discuss with friends and family the problems you and your spouse are having.

Involving friends and family prior to the actual divorce seems to force them to take sides, and yours may not be the side chosen. Also, letting other people into your marital problems can cause a bigger disaster if you and your spouse decide to work on staying married. Those people that you confided in may consider your spouse such a horrid person that they want nothing to do with him or her. They may confront your spouse with what you said and cause more problems. Many people consider confiding in others about the faults of their spouses one of the worst forms of betrayal, and betrayal is no way to begin rebuilding a marriage. Of course, if you must talk to someone make it a professional counselor or select one trusted person who will keep your confidences.

Social Life After Divorce

After your divorce, your social life will change. A strange thing happens to friends of a married couple when that couple gets a divorce. No matter how amicable the divorce, friends will take sides with one of the spouses. Just when both spouses could use the support of every friend, certain people will decide that they only want to be friendly with one spouse and will abandon the other. You may be considered as a threat to others' marriages, because you are no longer attached to one person or because you are free of the confines of marriage. You will become the odd man or woman out at dinner parties, the person everyone needs to fix up, and the envy of the unhappily married. Rest assured that you will make new friends, and there will be people who do not know you as part of a couple but as your own person.

Family

In most cases, a divorce will also mean that one side of your extended family no longer wants anything to do with you. Even in amicable divorces there can be hard feelings from the family of one of the spouses. To an adult, divorce may merely change where you celebrate the holidays. However, to children, being abandoned by part of their family can be devastating. If your holiday traditions change, make new traditions. If you have children, involve them in making new plans. Above all, be prepared to share the children with your ex-spouse's family.

Divorcing to Marry Another

One sad statistic is that the majority of those who get a divorce in order to marry another rarely end up marrying that person. This could be because of the extreme stress that going through a divorce causes or because of the guilt associated with being the person who has caused the breakup of a marriage. If you are the person who initiated the divorce in order to marry another, expect that there will be both guilt and stress. The carefree feelings of having an affair will be replaced by the reality of actually going through a divorce. This is a severe test of any relationship—especially a new one. If you are the other man or woman, you should expect that your lover will not be at his or her best during this time. It will be up to you to provide a very large portion of love and understanding in order to keep your relationship going.

Greed

There is something that happens to some people in the process of getting a divorce. They see all the stuff being divided and suddenly decide that they want it all. This is not uncommon—even the most agreeable couple who both want to get a divorce can be hit by greed. The problem comes when the greed leads to fraudulent actions or prolonging the finalization of the divorce.

Greed sometimes leads one spouse to selling off marital property or hiding it. Of course, this can become a criminal issue and cost the greedy spouse even more money. Another nasty action that comes out of greed is when both parties have agreed to all issues of the divorce and only one spouse has an attorney. The other represents him- or herself and trustingly signs the documents believing that they are exactly what had been agreed to. Sometimes it is only after the divorce is final that the nonrepresented spouse finds out that greed dictated a new agreement where he or she gets little or nothing.

In the case of divorce, greed is not good. If both spouses treat each other in a fair manner, the costs and the emotional upheaval of a divorce will be less.

Remember that going through a divorce can be devastating, but staying in a loveless marriage is much worse, lasts longer, and can literally waste the time you are alive.

COUNSELING

Few people can get through a divorce without professional help. This is especially true for children. Many counties in Illinois have plans to make professional counseling accessible to those who request it at reduced fees. You may even get your soon-to-be ex-spouse to agree to pay for professional counseling for the children as part of the settlement agreement. Some courts require professional counseling for children during a divorce; however, even if this is not a requirement, you may consider getting professional help for your children to ensure that they will adjust to the new lifestyle.

There are four primary goals of counseling during a divorce:

1.   to help you and your children through the breakup of the family;

2.   to help you deal with the stress of a major change in lifestyle;

3.   to help you rebuild your life as a productive member of society and a loving parent; and,

4.   to assist you and you spouse in determining if there is a chance for reconciliation.

Counseling ordered by the court is usually directed at the welfare of the children. It allows the children to talk about how your divorce affects them and gives them ways to express their feelings without taking sides. Many children also feel guilty about their role in the breakup of their parents' marriage. Counseling can get the children over the false idea that if they were just better kids their parents would still be together. It is very important to give your children the opportunity for counseling in a divorce situation, even if the court does not force you to do so.

For you, counseling can help you deal with your feelings of anger and inadequacy. If you have ever heard someone say that they keep selecting the wrong type of person, that is the kind of self-destructive pattern that counseling can address. You owe it to yourself to learn ways to deal with the anger and fear that most divorces bring.

FINANCIAL ASPECT OF DIVORCE

Divorcing costs money. Women do not make the same amount of salary as men. Recently, this unequal pay distribution has been expressed as for every dollar a man earns, a woman in the same job earns only sixty-three cents. Another fact is that most women will end up with custody of their children with men paying child support. What this means is that the family's earning power has dropped significantly due to the divorce.

Another fact that impacts the financial aspect of divorce is the length of time it takes to finish the process. The length of time for a divorce to be final depends on the details of each case, the children, property, cooperation of spouses, and the number of divorce cases on the court schedule (called the *docket*). Once a divorce has been filed, some spouses will do everything they can to delay the divorce from becoming final. In reality, delaying a divorce is only putting off the inevitable. It costs both parties unnecessary money and respect, and can cause numerous problems when children are involved. The spouse that purposely delays the inevitable divorce loses out both financially and on having any relationship with their former spouse and possibly their children.

While there is nothing one book can do to change these facts, this book provides information on the financial problems with divorce. The most important piece of information is a word of caution. Before you run out and file for a divorce, calmly and unemotionally take a long look at what a divorce will do to your financial life. You may find that because of financial needs, both you and your spouse should stay together. You may also find that counseling is much cheaper than a divorce lawyer. And for those who long for the carefree single life—as you get older, it becomes much more difficult to be carefree when most of your salary goes to child support.

Annulments and Legal Separations

Besides a divorce, there are two other ways in which a couple can legally end their relationship—an *annulment* and a *legal separation*. Both of these methods have their own requirements and restrictions.

ANNULMENT

A divorce legally breaks a valid marriage. An *annulment*, however, legally states that there was never a valid marriage. In Illinois, the courts enter a judgment declaring the marriage *invalid* and to this end have changed the name of the law from Annulment of Marriage to Invalidity of Marriage. (750 ILCS 5/301.) To prevent confusion, this book will continue to refer to this as an annulment.

An annulment is seldom used as a method to end a marriage because the grounds are generally harder to prove than the no-fault grounds for divorce. Where grounds for annulment clearly exist, this remedy results in neither party having a history of a divorce.

For anyone who is looking at an annulment for religious reasons, please note that this book only addresses a legal or state annulment—not a church annulment. Church annulments do not legally end marriages and do not have the power to provide for child or spousal support.

To obtain a religious annulment, you must go through a separate church procedure. You will need to consult your priest or minister for information on obtaining a church annulment, the church requirements as to the timing of obtaining a legal end to the marriage, and if you can get a church annulment after receiving a state divorce. Even if you do not plan to obtain a church annulment, consulting your priest or minister as part of planning to obtain a legal divorce may provide emotional support for you and your children.

Grounds for Annulment

There are only a few grounds available for annulment. Each of the grounds are discussed in the following paragraphs.

Lacked capacity to consent to marriage. Mental incapacity. A person who has a declared mental incapacity or infirmity does not have the legal ability to consent to marry. The courts construe this literally and look for a legal declaration of mental incapacity. This legal declaration is difficult to obtain and requires sworn testimony from doctors and a decision by a court.

Undue influence of alcohol, drugs, or other incapacitating substances. As a ground for an annulment, being under the influence of alcohol, drugs, or other incapacitating substances does not mean a person who is merely drunk or acting high. Courts require testimony that the person was so incapacitated that they were incoherent and did not know that they were being married. Again, a doctor's testimony and independent witness testimony may be required.

Induced to marry by force, duress, or fraud. Courts look at inducement by fraud as misrepresentation of the elements that are essential to a marriage. A situation in which a person lied about his or her ability to have sexual intercourse could be considered sufficient grounds to declare the marriage invalid. However, lies about fortune, character, or social status are not considered sufficient grounds, as these items are not essential to the marriage.

Lacked physical capacity to consummate marriage. If one person is physically unable to have sexual intercourse and the other party is not aware of this at the time of the marriage, the marriage can be declared invalid. The party who was not aware of this incapacity has one year to file for an annulment after obtaining this knowledge. This requires both elements—the physical inability of one party and the lack of knowledge of this inability by the other party. If both people know that their marriage can never be physically consummated and still marry, that marriage cannot be annulled or invalidated. Parties have ninety days to file for an annulment after they have knowledge of the lack of capacity.

One party is a minor and does not have parental or guardian's permission to marry. People aged 16 or 17 can marry *only* with the consent of their parents or guardian. (Those under age 16 are prohibited by law from marrying—even with consent.) Before the underage party reaches age 18, the marriage can be annulled or invalidated by either party or the minor's parents or guardians.

NOTE: *For the previous grounds, an annulment cannot be granted after one of the parties to the marriage has died.*

Marriage is invalid by law. Illinois Law 750 ILCS 5/212 lists those who are prohibited from marrying. This list includes:

- those who are already married;

- siblings;

- a parent and child;

- an uncle and niece;

- an aunt and nephew;

- first cousins; and,

- those of the same sex.

An annulment of the marriage of these people can be brought to court by either of the partners, the State's Attorney, or a child of either party up to three years after the death of the first party. If either of the parties to the invalid marriage was already legally married, the legal spouse can also file to obtain an annulment of the invalid marriage.

Annulments and Support

Unlike many other states, Illinois allows courts to award child support and maintenance in certain annulments. Courts look at each case on an individual basis in such awards.

In the case of *bigamy* (being married to several people at the same time), maintenance can be awarded to the person who in *good faith* married someone who was already married believing that this person was not already married. (*Good faith* means without knowledge of a violation of the law.) This requires that the spouse who is to receive the maintenance had absolutely no knowledge of the other person's valid marriage. Some courts have taken a hard line on this, and if there were obvious hints that the person was already married, these courts have denied maintenance.

Under the *Illinois Parentage Act of 1984*, all children have a right to monetary support by their parents regardless of whether the parents were in a valid marriage. (750 ILCS 45/1.) This right to monetary support also applies to parents who are themselves minors. Illinois courts have taken the stand that if a person is old enough to become a parent, then he or she is old enough to be required to support his or her child.

NOTE: *Because an annulment that includes child support or maintenance is complex, those seeking this should consider obtaining the assistance of an attorney.*

LEGAL SEPARATION

A *legal separation* is *not* the first step to getting a divorce. In reality, this is a rarely used procedure. In fact, most family law professionals will advise a couple not to pursue a legal separation unless there are special circumstances. These special circumstances can be in the area of religious prohibitions to being divorced or a personal conviction not to be divorced. In the case of special circumstances, the reason to obtain a legal separation is to get court-ordered child support or maintenance from a spouse who has left the marital home to live elsewhere. However, there are other, less expensive methods to obtain these same results.

The procedures for obtaining a legal separation are almost identical to obtaining a divorce. (750 ILCS 5/402.) The costs of getting a legal separation can be as high or higher than getting a divorce, and you are still legally married.

In order to qualify to file for a legal separation, the couple must already be living *separate and apart*. Separate and apart is a legal term that some courts have interpreted to include living in the same house but not in the same bed, or living in separate areas of the same building.

The person who files for the legal separation must be without fault in the breakup of the marriage. However, the courts do not require total blamelessness. What they are looking for is that the filing spouse did not consent to the separation, had not failed to perform a marital duty, or was not guilty of misconduct, which materially caused the breakup of the marriage. This means that the spouse who has taken on a lover, the spouse who has moved out of the marital home, or the spouse who has in any way violated the marriage vows, should *not* be the one to file for a legal separation.

In the real world, since marriages are usually in trouble because of the actions of *both* parties, it may be difficult to determine which spouse should file for legal separation. In most cases, the spouse who remains in the marital home, the spouse who has responsibility for the children, or the spouse who will receive support payments is the one to file for a separation.

A judgment of the court for legal separation will *not* dissolve the marriage. This means that property obtained after a legal separation may be considered a *marital asset* if the couple does get a divorce.

A court usually will not make a determination of ownership of assets in a legal separation on its own. The court will, however, approve of a written division of assets or settlement agreement that is approved by both parties. This means that when filing for a legal separation, the couple should include a written settlement agreement that covers the division of all marital assets, just as when filing for a divorce. (See Chapter 11 for information on settlement agreements.) Courts will make determinations regarding child custody, child support, and spousal maintenance in a legal separation.

NOTE: *Obtaining a judgment of legal separation does not prevent either party from filing for a divorce.*

Why Use a Legal Separation

In a legal separation, you and your spouse make a formal agreement as to who pays for what, the custody of the children, and other important items. That agreement is then filed with the court, which can enforce it. Many times, couples will decide to enter into such an agreement to guarantee that their finances will be properly handled before attempting counseling or as an emotional step prior to divorce. Other couples may need a legal separation rather than a divorce due to financial reasons. The major financial reasons for using a legal separation are:

- ✪ taxes may be less on separated couples;

- ✪ if the nonemployee spouse has a preexisting medical condition, the couple may need to remain legally married in order to continue medical insurance coverage;

- ✪ the couple may need to remain married due to the ten-year Social Security benefit requirement; or,

- ✪ the couple may need to remain married due to the twenty-year requirement for both spouses to have PX and commissary benefits in a military marriage.

Separation Agreements

In order for a Separation Agreement to be binding, it must be filed with the court. (More on Courts and Forms in Chapter 8.) The Separation Agreement must be something that both you and your spouse have negotiated and both of you agree to. It should be a concise agreement, written as a court order.

At minimum, your Separation Agreement should contain information covering the following areas.

✪ *Child support payments*. How much is paid? When it is paid?

✪ *Child custody*. Who do the children live with?

✪ *Visitation*. Set a fair visitation schedule. Include items such as holidays, birthdays, how to handle changes, and how to deal with school events.

✪ *Marital home*. Who lives there? How are the bills paid? Who pays for emergency repairs?

✪ *Bills*. Who pays for bills?

✪ *Taxes*. Who gets child and mortgage deductions? How is a refund or a tax bill handled?

✪ *Maintenance or alimony*. Who will be paying and how much, how often?

The Legal System

Since divorce is a legal procedure, you need to be aware of how the legal system works. This means you need a basic understanding of the laws, procedures, and rules that must be followed in a divorce case.

For example, parties must file for a divorce in the county in which they reside. Residence is extremely important in a divorce. You must be a resident of Illinois for ninety days prior to filing for a divorce in this state. Residence is also referred to as your *domicile*, which is the place that you live and intend to live in for the foreseeable future, no matter if your residence is your choice or directed by military service.

There are some divorce cases in which the majority of court action has been to determine residence. For most people, residence is not a question. It is the home where that person lives, where he or she votes, where his or her mail is delivered, and the location considered as his or her primary residence by the IRS.

This chapter covers how you can learn more about these laws and procedures, and provides some information about finding and researching them.

RESEARCH

The laws are called *statutes*. Annotated statutes will have some cases that are the best examples of the law attached to each statute. Illinois has many statutes that cover divorce. The primary ones are found in Chapter 325 Children and Chapter 750:

- ✪ Act 5 Illinois Marriage and Dissolution of Marriage Act;

- ✪ Act 10 Illinois Uniform Premarital Agreement Act;

- ✪ Act 16 Non-Support Punishment Act;

- ✪ Act 22 Uniform Interstate Family Support Act;

- ✪ Act 25 Expedited Child Support Act of 1990;

- ✪ Act 28 Income Withholding for Support Act;

- ✪ Act 35 Uniform Child Custody Jurisdiction Act;

- ✪ Act 40 Illinois Parentage Act; and,

- ✪ Act 45 Illinois Parentage Act of 1984.

Most people find the wording of these laws tedious and vague. If your divorce is becoming so complex that you are attempting to read these statutes, that is probably a sign that you need to get the help of an experienced family law attorney. Some of the more useful statutes are reproduced in the back of this book. It is strongly suggested that you review these and the other Illinois laws before attempting to act as your own attorney. For a person who just wants to know if they can get a divorce, the simple statute without the key cases is probably sufficient.

Cases are listed in digests. However, only cases that rise to the appellate level are printed. The majority of cases are simply in court files, filed by parties' names, dates, and court that made the decision.

Remember, if you feel that your case is so complex that you are asking the librarian for hard-to-read legal treatises, you probably should turn your case over to an attorney. Generally, your research needs can be met by looking at the statutes and the wealth of information on the Internet.

The Internet   The Internet has become a valuable source of information in our society. There are many sites directed at increasing the public's knowledge of legal documents. Many of the bar associations, such as the American Bar Association, provide helpful information and links to other information sites. However, there are problems with Internet sites. There is no guarantee that the information posted is correct or even the current law. Also, no Internet site can answer all of your questions on getting a divorce—that personalized service can only be obtained from an attorney who practices family law.

The following Internet sites have been around for some time and should be reliable places to begin research. These sites provide links to several additional sources of information and points of research. Remember, you can always do an Internet search on words like "Illinois divorce," "divorce," or other specific terms.

- ✪ American Bar Association at **www.abanet.org**

- ✪ DuPage County Bar Association at **www.dcba.org**

- ✪ Illinois State Bar Association at **www.isba.org**

- ✪ Legal Research sites:

  - **www.divorcelawinfo.com**

  - **www.findlaw.com**

  - **www.lawguru.com**

  - **www.law.com**

- ✪ State of Illinois at **www.state.il.us.gov**

- ✪ Cook County Clerk of Court (includes forms) at **www.cook countyclerkofcourt.org**

- ✪ DuPage County Clerk of Court (includes forms) at **www.dupageco.org/courtclerk**

- ✪ General divorce help:

  - **www.divorceHQ.com**

  - **www.divorceinfo.com**

  - **www.divorcemag.com**

  - **www.divorcenet.com**

  - **www.divorcesource.com**

  - **www.divorcesupport.com**

In recent years there has been a flood of great websites about handling divorce. These come from two groups. The first group is the family law attorneys who want to represent you in your divorce. These attorneys are willing to provide online information on divorcing in Illinois for free. Yes, they are giving information away. Many of these attorneys can be found through the Internet locations previously provided.

The second group of great websites for those interested in divorce is coming from the clerks of the Circuit Courts. Appendix A provides a list of addresses, phone numbers, and Internet sites for the Circuit Courts in Illinois. Not every Circuit Court has a website, but more are developing one all the time. In Chapter 8, the forms the Circuit Court websites provide are discussed in detail.

Libraries   Even in this computer society, laws and legal help are still printed in books. Many local libraries have the current Illinois Statutes in printed format. There are also law libraries that the public can use. These law libraries are located in law schools and at the majority of Circuit Court buildings. Librarians, especially those in law libraries, are usually extremely helpful to the public.

Besides the actual printed laws, there are also books that will assist you in understanding the laws. Most libraries have public computers so you can also review the Internet sites listed.

COUNTY CIRCUIT COURTS

For the majority of people, you will need to make at least one court appearance in order to obtain your divorce. It makes sense for you to know a little about the court system.

Illinois involves several levels of government in divorces. The state laws govern the grounds for getting a divorce, what is marital property, who gets custody of the children, and the amount of child support. These four items, among many others, are predetermined by laws enacted by the state's elected officials.

The court that hears the petition for the divorce and determines what procedure the parties must use to obtain a divorce is called the Circuit Court. There are twenty-two circuits in Illinois. Three circuits are single-county circuits—Cook County, DuPage County, and Will County. The other nineteen circuits contain multiple counties, and therefore, multiple buildings called the Circuit Court. More information on the Circuit Courts is in Appendix A, or you can look them up on the Internet at **www.state.il.us/court/CircuitCourts**.

Within the Circuit Court system there are a large number of courtrooms and judges that are regularly assigned to divorces. Your local county may refer to these particular courtrooms as divorce courts, domestic relations courts, or family courts. One of the primary reasons that the court system that handles divorces is kept separate from other legal cases is for the protection of and assistance to the parties divorcing. Many of the courtroom workers are experienced in dealing with divorce cases and are able to provide better assistance to the divorcing parties than those who deal with non-family law cases.

The Courtroom   The layout of each courtroom may vary, but they all have a few common items. The judge sits behind a desk or bench at the end of the room. To his or her immediate right or left is a courtroom clerk. A bailiff or sheriff may be close to the clerk.

In front of the judge there may be two tables, one for each side of a lawsuit. You and your attorney (if you have one) may sit at one of these tables, which face the judge. When it is your turn the clerk or the judge will call your case. At that point, you stand up in front of the judge to answer his or her questions. Some courtrooms have a podium between the tables. In that case, you would speak from the podium instead of walking up to the judge.

People Involved in a Court Case

There are several people involved in a divorce case besides you and your spouse.

Judge. The judge presides over the courtroom and makes the final decisions about your divorce. The judge also approves any settlement you and your spouse may reach, and any decisions regarding minor children.

Always rise when the judge enters the courtroom. When addressing the judge call him or her "your honor," "sir," or "ma'am." Do not talk back, yell, curse, or talk over the judge.

Attorney. An attorney represents someone with legal problems. He or she acts on your behalf in court, can negotiate settlements, and can help you with your case. See Chapter 4 for more information on attorneys.

Circuit clerk. The circuit clerk is an elected management position. Each county has at least one circuit clerk who is responsible for handling the court files. For most courts, you will see many other people who are also identified as clerks. These people care for court files, help people file new cases, and process judicial orders. While the clerks cannot give you legal assistance, they can help you understand the procedure needed to file a case.

The clerks who file the cases and deal with the court files can be a wealth of information. Remember, they have a high-stress job dealing with tons of paper and the public. Be kind, and treat these people with respect and dignity, no matter how frustrated you are.

Court clerks. Within the courtroom, most judges will have a judicial clerk who assists with calling the cases and making sure the court file is kept complete. These people can also be a wealth of information. Besides knowing the law of the courtroom, they can tell you what procedure the judge follows, what time of the day you can speak with the judge, and what forms to file. Again, the court clerks cannot assist you with legal advice, so do not embarrass yourself by asking. As with the other clerks in the court system, court clerks should also be treated with dignity and respect.

NOTE: *A general rule when dealing with anyone who works within the court system is to use the terms "please," "thank you," "sir," and "ma'am."*

Judge's secretary or clerk. You may encounter a person called the judge's secretary or even the judge's clerk if you have a meeting with the judge in his or her chambers (office). This person works directly for that judge, and handles the judge's appointments or other clerical work. In a divorce, it is not unusual for a judge to ask to speak to one of the parties, both parties, the attorneys, or even the children in his or her chambers. Conversations in the chambers can be recorded by a court stenographer or can just be a private conversation.

Court reporter or court stenographer. Most courts that hear divorces will employ a court reporter or stenographer to record the proceeding. In some of the newer courts the proceedings are recorded on tiny microphones and transcribed by stenographers in another location. No matter how it is recorded, you may be asked to spell names and uncommon words so that the stenographer can transcribe your testimony correctly.

Whenever speaking to the judge in a courtroom, speak clearly, do not mumble, and speak loud enough to be heard. Because some courtrooms have microphones placed within the courtroom, once the proceedings have started, stop all conversations until you appear in front of the judge.

Bailiff or sheriff. Courtrooms, especially those where divorces are heard, usually have at least one uniformed bailiff or sheriff. Their duty is to keep the peace and enforce the law within the courtroom. Outside the courtroom they also serve, or give people legal notices (summons) that they are being sued.

In courtrooms, it is the bailiff or sheriff who keeps order. He or she may enforce a *no talking rule* during the proceedings or other rules of the court. Pay proper respect to this person just as you would the policeman on the street—both can put you in jail.

Mediator. A judge may order divorcing parties to see a mediator. A *mediator* is a neutral person who can assist you and your spouse to come to an agreement. A mediator is not a judge, but assists the court by helping divorcing parties to reach a mutual agreement. In many divorce cases involving minor children, a mediator is appointed by the judge. After a mediator meets with the parties, he or she will report back to the judge.

Mediators do not take sides in a divorce. That is a fact. Their job is to listen to both sides and help both people come to an agreement. Refusing to cooperate with court-ordered mediation or accusing your mediator of only supporting your spouse will cause you problems with the judge. Remember, the judge sent you to the mediator because he or she wanted you and your spouse to work out an agreement together instead of having the court impose an agreement on you.

Counselor. A judge may also order divorcing parties to see a counselor individually or in the context of parenting classes. More courts are requiring that divorcing parents of minor children attend these sessions. It is important for your children that you put forth the effort to attend and cooperate in these sessions.

TEN TIPS FOR
APPEARING IN COURT ON A DIVORCE

1. Try to settle as much as possible with your spouse before going before the judge.

2. If using an attorney, let your attorney speak for you. Do not interrupt your attorney, even if what he or she said bothers you.

3. Follow the instructions that your attorney has given you. Your attorney will have a strategy to win this case, and if you go against that strategy you may endanger the case.

4. Speak respectfully to the judge. Do not interrupt the judge, even if what he or she says upsets you.

5. Do not expect that the judge will always side with you. If the judge rules against you, do not make a scene.

6. Be prepared by bringing all the documents and information that you were asked to bring into the court.

7. Bring a pad of paper and pen to take notes. Use this to write down the comments of your attorney, the judge, and the other side that bother you. After the court appearance, speak to your attorney about these.

8. Do not make hostile comments, faces, audible sighs, or gestures to your spouse, your spouse's attorney, or the judge.

9. Do not take children into the courtroom unless told to do so by your attorney or the judge. Many courthouses have a children's room where children can be left with supervision supplied by the court.

10. Dress appropriately. Show respect for the court and the judge by dressing for a business event in your *Sunday best*. This means leaving flip-flops, midriff-bearing tops, cut-offs, sheer tops, shorts, and anything ripped or dirty at home.

Attorneys

A divorce is an expensive and difficult legal procedure, even ignoring all the emotions it stirs up. As a legal procedure, each and every issue can produce a series of complex court responses. Each child, each piece of property, the division of income, and the visitation schedule, can create many decisions that must be resolved to the court's satisfaction. It may be your first experience with the legal system—a system that is complex, slow, and at times may seem unfair.

Attorneys who handle divorces are commonly called *family law attorneys*. Illinois does not license *specialties* (state-recognized specialists) in family law. However, some attorneys and law firms do limit their practice to the area of family law.

NEEDING AN ATTORNEY

A rule of thumb for those who are attempting to handle their own legal work in a divorce is to hire an attorney if:

- ✪ your spouse hires an attorney;

- ✪ there are children and child support involved;

✪ you want to get spousal maintenance;

✪ there is spousal abuse (physical or mental) involved;

✪ your spouse is noncooperative; or,

✪ you feel that you are overwhelmed with the divorce procedure.

FINDING AN ATTORNEY

Choosing an attorney can be confusing. Many people rely on referrals from family, friends, or business associates, such as your investment broker, insurance broker, or bank. You can also obtain referrals from local, county, or state bar associations. There are some attorneys who limit their practice to handling divorce and child custody for husbands, and others who limit their practice to representing the wives. The majority of family law attorneys are not that limited and will represent either side. Many of the limited associations or law firms will advertise in the Yellow Pages or on the Internet.

Beware of attorneys who encourage or motivate the client to act on revenge against his or her spouse. A spouse who wants revenge can prolong a divorce for years and increase legal fees. An example is the spouse who continues to argue about a property settlement for so long that he or she must sell the home to pay legal fees once the divorce is final. Revenge can sometimes result in one spouse doing an illegal act. Spouses who illegally destroy marital or the other spouse's personal property are not helping themselves in a divorce action, especially when custody or visitation of children is involved.

An honest attorney will steer the client in the direction of a fair settlement for all parties. A *fair settlement* means that both sides give and take. No one gets 100% of what they want.

Whatever way you select an attorney to assist you in obtaining a divorce, make sure that this attorney is familiar with the complex and fast-changing area of family law in your county.

As you evaluate several law firms and attorneys, you may want to keep track of certain issues to help you pick the right attorney for you. You may want to use the following Attorney Checklist for that evaluation. Make copies of this checklist and use one for each attorney you speak to. Once you have contacted several attorneys, you can evaluate them on the same important criteria.

ATTORNEY CHECKLIST

Name of Attorney: _____

Referred by: _____

Law Firm Address: _____

_____

_____

Phone Number: _____

Fax Number: _____

Hours (when can attorney meet with you): _____

Approximate cost for divorce: _____

Cost for phone calls: _____

Policy on returning client calls: _____

_____

Additional costs: _____

_____

How long does average divorce take? _____

How many divorce cases has attorney handled? _____

What should I know about your law firm handling my divorce?

_____

_____

UNDERSTANDING COSTS

The financial effects of a divorce will be with you for the rest of your life. Your credit, your children, and your family will be effected. This is a major event in your life, and major life events can be expensive. However, there are some things that you can do to keep attorney expenses down, and because there are a number of family law attorneys licensed in Illinois, you are likely to get someone who is in your price range.

The first step, of course, is to shop around for an attorney who meets your legal and financial criteria. This may require calls to several law firms inquiring about their services, their experience in family law, and their costs. Attorneys are usually not able to give you a precise cost of a divorce case over the phone, since they need to look at the case and determine how much time it may take.

Most law firms will require a *retainer*, which is an amount of money given in advance that the firm will apply to the bills on a particular schedule. Many firms will bill all the work done on a case against the retainer on a monthly basis. If the amount of work done exceeds the amount provided for in a retainer, the firm will require additional funds.

Some firms will charge a flat amount (or fixed fee) for a divorce, which is also paid in advance. However, even those who charge a flat amount may have a provision for additional charges or expenses in association with obtaining a divorce.

For both firms that use the retainer system and those that charge flat amounts, the charges are calculated by the hours spent by the attorney, paralegal, law clerk, or other staff multiplied by the hourly rate for that person. Other charges are expenses such as court filing fees, charges for having paperwork served, and different expenses in association with the divorce.

The amount of retainer and hourly rates should be spelled out in a contract, usually called the *client-attorney representation agreement*. No matter what it is called, it should list how costs are calculated, and if there is a retainer or flat charge. It should be signed and dated by both the client and the attorney.

NOTE: *If a law firm is reluctant to give you a copy of this agreement to look over before you sign, find another law firm.*

Keeping Legal Costs Down

At your first meeting with an attorney, you should be honest about your ability to pay and the limits of your budget. Let the attorney know the extent that you are willing to assist in keeping the costs down. Some attorneys will welcome a client who is willing to perform some of the legwork. Others have a tight system that is efficient as it stands. All attorneys will welcome a client who is honest about finances and will not waste the attorney's time.

A good way to keep costs down is to be prepared for all meetings with your attorney. Do not wait until the last minute to gather information, copies of documents, or a list of questions for your meetings with your attorney. A client who comes prepared to meetings with information and promptly provides documents when asked to do so conveys the message that he or she will not pay for wasted time.

Many family law attorneys limit or charge for questions from clients. While this may seem especially mean, it is done so that the attorney is not spending all of his or her time on the phone with the client who has the fastest speed dial. You should ask your attorney about his or her policy on questions from clients. Some questions can be answered by the paralegal, law clerk, or secretary, and do not have to go to the attorney. It is in your financial interest to limit your calls to your attorney to important matters. Before calling, gather together all issues and questions. You may wish to write everything down you want to discuss with your attorney so that you can efficiently use the time allotted to you.

Qualifying for Free Legal Help

Many bar associations and legal aid associations help people who need legal assistance but cannot afford to pay. In general, only those who qualify under the *Federal Poverty Guidelines* will be eligible for these programs. The Federal Poverty Guidelines are issued annually, and can be obtained at your local library and from local assistance agencies. If you qualify for state or local assistance, such as food stamps or rental assistance, you may also qualify under these guidelines. Some Circuit Courts allow a person to file as *indigent* with proof that he or she qualifies under these guidelines (contact the clerk of the Circuit Court in your county). Many of these programs are specifically for the elderly, disabled, military, or people in special circumstances (such as in the case of a natural disaster, those with breast cancer, or victims of domestic violence).

NOTE: *Several bar associations and agencies are providing legal help for those in the military. Many of these programs are free to the service person and are run by volunteer attorneys.*

If you think you may qualify for free or reduced-rate legal services, it is up to you to do some research and be prepared to prove that you qualify. If your income is below the federal poverty guidelines and you are getting state or local assistance, check with the office that is providing this assistance for legal referrals. Others should begin with their local community.

Many community-based programs offer limited services to residents. Start with your city, town, or suburb, then go on to the county services, and then to the state services. Look in phone books, local directories, state program directories, and federal program directories for references such as "lawyer referral services," "legal aid," "free legal hotlines," or "pro bono legal services." Some local law schools also provide low-cost services done by the students and supervised by licensed attorneys. Local and national bar associations may also provide referrals to low-cost attorneys who are members of their association.

The largest bar association in the country is the American Bar Association. There is a state Illinois Bar Association, local city associations such as the Chicago Bar Association, county associations such as DuPage County Bar Association, and numerous others. Almost every county in Illinois has its own bar association. Many of the organizations and bar associations maintain websites on the Internet. One notable site is the one provided by the American Bar Association, **www.abanet.org**, which has a section on obtaining free legal help. Other websites are listed in the research section of Chapter 3.

WHAT TO BRING TO YOUR
FIRST MEETING WITH AN ATTORNEY

When you set up an initial meeting with an attorney, you may be asked to bring certain documents, information, and possibly a check for the initial consultation fee. Make sure that you know what documents and information you are being asked for and that what you provide is both current and accurate. If you agree to meet with an attorney who requires an initial consultation fee, please remember to bring the money with you. By bringing all that you were asked for, you are sending a message that you will cooperate with the attorney to move the case along.

Most counties in Illinois require that those being divorced fill out a court-ordered *financial disclosure form*. Your attorney will provide you with the correct form for your county. This form lists the assets and debts of each party to the marriage. You will be signing under oath that the information provided to the court is correct, so do not lie on this form.

There are also worksheets in Appendix C that will help you in preparing any financial disclosure form. (see page 207.) Take the time to fill in the information on these worksheets before you meet with an attorney. You will save both the attorney and yourself time at your meetings. Some law firms and some courts will require this information put in a different order, but if you have all of the information with you, that will be an easy task.

CHECKLIST OF DOCUMENTS NEEDED
FOR THE FIRST MEETING
WITH AN ATTORNEY

❑   For all former spouses: name; date of birth; if deceased, date of death; if divorced, date of divorce and the state where the divorce was granted; any court-ordered financial support; and, children from each prior marriage

❑   If you have lived or have property in a *community property* (share all property 50/50) state (Arizona, California, Idaho, Louisiana, Nevada, New Mexico, Texas, or Washington), bring copies of the deed to the property

❑   Copies of current wills, trusts, powers of attorney

❑   Financial statements from businesses you or your spouse own

❑   Copies of deeds to property

❑   Retirement benefit summary

❑   Life insurance information

❑   Prenuptial agreements

❑   Postnuptial agreements

❑   Records of stock, business interests, and other assets

❑   Copies of IRS income tax documents

Your attorney will ask you for lots of personal and financial information. Respond honestly. Information given to your attorney is held in confidence by law. Have and discuss your objectives with your attorney. (Do you want custody? Do you want certain marital property?) Cover all your concerns with your attorney. Insist on clarification of any legal issues that you do not understand. It is also a very good idea to take notes at every meeting and phone conversation with your attorney, especially the initial consultation.

Above all, if you hire an attorney, *follow your attorney's advice.* Clients who ask their attorney for advice and then do not follow it are wasting both their money and their attorney's time. There is nothing more frustrating and more detrimental to a good attorney-client relationship than a client who ignores or acts against his or her attorney's direction.

FAMILY LAW ATTORNEYS

It takes a special person to become a family law attorney because this is such an emotionally draining field. The family law attorney hears about failed marriages, mental cruelty, physical abuse, and broken hearts every day. Think of how it would be to spend all of your working hours listening to and trying to help people with marital problems.

Most family law attorneys cope with this constant parade of sadness by keeping a demeanor of emotional detachment and limiting their time discussing the emotional side of the divorce. This does not necessarily mean that the attorney does not care about your case, but he or she must convince a judge to rule in your favor, and judges in divorce court are not swayed by emotions. They deal in fact and law, no matter how severe the abuse and no matter how shocking the actions of one spouse.

PROBLEMS WITH YOUR ATTORNEY

If it seems that the court is taking too long in granting your divorce or if the court rules against you, your first inclination may be to blame the attorney. In reality, many problems can be due to a court that has too many cases or a judge who has an overbooked calendar. The judge him- or herself can be very thorough, reviewing every document, making sure everything submitted to the court withstands rigorous examination to prevent his or her decision from being overturned. Judges may rule against you on motions or at hearings. These things and others are beyond the control of any attorney. The financial truth is that attorneys want their cases to be fairly and quickly decided so that they can work on the next case.

Look at your expectations. Your divorce is not like your cousin's or your next-door neighbor's. Every divorce is unique and has its own set of problems. The client who demands to know why her attorney cannot get her maintenance of $5,000 a month like the attorney got for her best friend needs to understand the unique situation in each divorce. For one, the best friend may be stretching the truth or leaving out a crucial part of the agreement.

Some problems are misunderstandings that can be quickly resolved. If the problem is that your attorney will not return your calls, send a certified letter requesting that he or she call you. If your attorney works in a large law firm, he or she may be working under a senior attorney or partner who may be able to assist you. If the problem is that you are unhappy with the decision made by the family law court, ask to meet with your attorney so that he or she can explain the decision and advise you of any future options. Set up this meeting as a professional appointment, and offer to pay for your attorney's time.

Fire Your Attorney

If you still believe that you have serious problems with your attorney, consider filing a complaint against him or her, or firing this attorney and retaining another. Remember, if you do fire your attorney, you will still be legally liable for all legal fees incurred up to that point. Some attorneys will not take a case that has been started by another attorney; those who do may require an additional fee for reviewing a prior attorney's work.

NOTE: *Unfortunately, as with every occupation, there are a few attorneys who do act fraudulently, and these few should be reported to the Attorney Registration and Disciplinary Commission (ARDC) of the Supreme Court of Illinois. The ARDC has offices in both Chicago and Springfield, and can be found in the phone book or by contacting Information.*

Move to Another Attorney

In law school, professors say that if you put ten attorneys in a room and gave them a legal problem, you would end up with ten different solutions to the same problem and none of the solutions would be wrong. That is the way it is with law—most of it is not black and white, but is varying shades of gray. Family law is full of these gray shades. This is different from what you see on TV, when the bad guy gets caught and goes to jail, all in sixty minutes with commercials. In family situations there seldom are real bad guys, just people who have decided to move on and the children who get caught up in the push-pull of parents wanting a divorce.

There are some clients who retain an attorney, disagree with what the attorney has done, then gets another attorney until that attorney disagrees with the client, and so on. It is not unusual to hear about people involved in a lengthy divorce who have gone through several attorneys. The problem with this is that it will cause delays in getting your divorce and will certainly cost you more money. Clients who routinely use and then discard their attorneys can represent a red flag for many attorneys, because there is a fear that nothing will ever satisfy this client. Such a client may have a lot of difficulty even finding a new lawyer to take his or her case.

While a client certainly has the legal right to change lawyers at any time, before making such a change look at your situation and ask yourself some questions. Was this really the attorney's problem or did the problem originate with the judge? How much money do you owe this attorney? Is this merely a personality conflict between you an your attorney? Have you spoken to your attorney about this? Are you being forced to compromise (usually a direction of the court)? Are you taking your anger against you spouse out on your attorney? Are you angry because you do not want a divorce? How much money are you willing to invest in a new lawyer? Do you have another lawyer who will take on the case?

If you feel confident that you have real reasons to look for another attorney, you may want to speak to another attorney who will merely review your case, for a fee. This would give you a neutral opinion on your case.

Protecting Yourself and Your Children

Many marriages are plagued with domestic violence. Physical and mental abuse is not acceptable and it is illegal. Domestic violence is not only a problem in a marriage—it can rob your children of their childhood. This chapter is for those who have problems with domestic violence, even if you are not planning a divorce.

DOMESTIC VIOLENCE

The state of Illinois takes the issue of domestic violence very seriously and has passed several laws addressing this issue. The primary law is the *Illinois Domestic Violence Act of 1986*. (750 ILCS 60.) This law provides the procedure for obtaining *orders of protection* and the enforcement of these orders. It also allows enforcement of orders of protection that are issued in other states.

Under Illinois law, domestic violence includes physical abuse, threats of physical harm, unlawful imprisonment, harassment, stalking, intimidation of a dependent, or interference with personal liberty. The abuser can be a spouse, ex-spouse, boyfriend, girlfriend, casual date, someone you formerly lived with, a blood relation, a relation by marriage, a caregiver, or someone with whom you have had a child. This law allows the person who is abused to get a court order of protection against the abuser.

The court Order of Protection is designed to stop the violence by limiting the abuser's access to his or her victim. There are three types of protection orders available in Illinois: an *Emergency Order* or *Temporary Order*, an *Interim Order*, and a *Plenary Order*.

Emergency and Temporary Orders

A *temporary restraining order* (TRO) can be obtained in emergency situations when one spouse can prove that there is an urgent need to stop the other spouse from doing something or acting in a way that will result in permanent injury or serious loss. Emergency situations can be such things as a threatened physical attack, destruction of marital assets, or potential removal of a child from the court's jurisdiction.

NOTE: *Any restraining order is merely a piece of paper without a guarantee. Many women who have obtained valid restraining orders against ex-husbands end up being harmed again by these same men. There are organizations and private attorneys who concentrate on assisting victims of domestic violence in obtaining a divorce and getting the appropriate level of protection.*

Interim Order

Like the temporary order, an *interim order of protection* is issued when a judge is convinced that harm will come to you if the order is not granted. For an interim order, the abuser will be notified. Interim orders usually last up to thirty days and may be extended after a full hearing regarding the abuse. As with all orders of protection, a court clerk can advise you about what form you will need to file.

Plenary Order

A *plenary order of protection* is only issued with the permission of a judge after a full hearing. At the hearing, the abuser will be allowed to tell his or her side. This order of protection may last up to two years, but the victim, with permission of the court, can renew it.

How to Get an Order of Protection

To obtain an Order of Protection you will need to go to a Circuit Court in the county you live in and request a petition for one of the mentioned orders. You will fill out the petition, and a judge will review your petition, ask you questions, and then decide if he or she approves the petition. You will then need to get a copy of the order signed by the judge served on the abuser. Sheriffs, police, and process servers will do this for a fee. Do not attempt to give your abuser a copy of the order in person.

If the protection order requires a hearing, the judge will set the time and date of this hearing. You must go to the hearing. If you do not show up, the order will be dismissed. At the hearing, you must prove that the abuser did the things you accused him or her of, and that you need the protection of the court. You prove your case by bringing in witnesses or showing written documentation of abuse. Written evidence can be medical reports, police reports, pictures of your injuries, lists of calls to 911, and any other information that will support you.

If your abuser has retained an attorney, you should also get an attorney. This may mean that you ask the court to continue the case until you can retain an attorney.

Court Hearing for an Order of Protection

A hearing for an order of protection is the same as other court hearings. The hearing is held in a courtroom and is presided over by a judge, who makes a decision. Once your case is called, you and the abuser will come in front of the judge. The court clerk will swear in all witnesses and you will get the opportunity to present your case. If you have an attorney, this will be done by the attorney asking you and then the abuser questions. If an attorney does not represent you, you will just tell your side to the judge, who may or may not ask questions. The judge will then make a decision as to issuing the Order of Protection.

Once You Get an Order of Protection

The first thing you do is to make several copies of this order. Keep a copy with you at all times. Give a copy to your employer (this may mean giving a copy to the receptionist), the guard, Human Resources, your supervisor, and your manager. Give a copy to your local law enforcement. Give a copy to your children's school or day care. Keep a copy in your car. You may also want to give copies to neighbors, close friends, and relatives, so that they can help look out for you.

Remember the Order of Protection is just a piece of paper. It is up to you to keep yourself out of harm's way. That may mean moving to a secure location, changing locks on your home, installing an alarm system, and altering your routine so that your abuser cannot keep track of you.

What to Do if the Abuser Violates the Order

If your abuser violates an Order of Protection, immediately call the police, even for minor infractions. Once the police show up, let them see the Order of Protection and make sure that a police report is filed even if no arrest is made.

Assistance from the Internet

The subject of domestic violence is very serious and could take an entire book to thoroughly present. Luckily, information is readily available on the Internet. The following are some very good websites that provide information on preventing and stopping domestic abuse.

- Illinois Coalition Against Domestic Violence—**www.ilcadv.org**. On this website, you can find the nearest agency to assist you and copies of orders of protection.

- National Domestic Violence Hotline—**www.ndvh.org**. This is the agency that operates the hotline 800-799-SAFE (7233), which runs twenty-four hours a day in more than 140 languages.

- WomensLaw.org—**www.womenslaw.org**. This site provides legal information by state for teens, immigrants, and the military. It also assists with security and safety planning, and the issues of custody and kidnapping.

- Feminist Majority Foundation—**www.feminist.org**. Contains information on problems faced by all women, including domestic violence.

- End Abuse—**www.endabuse.org**. Provides information on training young people to respect women.

CHILD ABUSE

Along with the issue of domestic violence is the very real atrocity of child abuse. Children are often caught up in the anger and revenge that comes along with an abusive marriage. Parents are the primary protectors of the innocent children, but everyone has the responsibility to prevent child abuse. Illinois law allows restraining orders and orders of protection against a parent who is abusing his or her children. Additionally, Illinois criminalizes child abuse and aggressively prosecutes both parents and non-parents for such abuse. Illinois has enacted the *Abuse and Neglected Child Reporting Act*, which requires the Department of Children & Family Services (DCFS) to investigate and prosecute child abuse. (325 ILCS 5.) This law also requires those who routinely deal with children (such as teachers, medical personnel, etc.) to report any indication of child abuse.

If you are unsure of who you should call, some national organizations may be able to assist you. Some nationwide contacts include 800-4-A-CHILD, 800-CHILDREN, and **www.preventchilabuse.org**. If you cannot get anyone to help or if the child is in immediate danger, contact your local police department.

Divorce Basics

Courts demand that the spouse who files for a divorce provide a reason for wanting that divorce. While all married people can at one time or another do something that will make their spouse think about a divorce, courts demand that actual legal reasons be used when filing for a divorce. These legal reasons are called *grounds*.

GROUNDS

When one spouse has been wronged by the other spouse's cheating, it is very easy for the wronged spouse to take any opportunity to get revenge. A common way is to charge *adultery*, because that will prove to family and friends that he or she was the wronged party.

The reality of the situation is that this country no longer brands people if they have sex with someone other than their spouse. The divorce papers that contain the details of the adultery end up left in the courthouse files, where few people will ever view the result. As for the court, the fact is that the spousal fault and misconduct only means less chance for settling the case in a friendly manner. Technically, Illinois has two types of grounds for divorce—*fault* and *irreconcilable differences*.

Fault Grounds   Illinois statute defines eleven *fault grounds* used in filing for a divorce. (750 ILCS 5/401(a)(1).) These are:

1. being unable to have sexual intercourse at the time of marriage and during the term of the marriage;

2. bigamy;

3. adultery;

4. desertion (absent one year including time case is pending);

5. habitual drunkenness for two years;

6. gross and confirmed habits caused by the excessive use of addictive drugs for two years (use of such drugs became a controlling or dominant purpose in that person's life);

7. attempt on the life of the other spouse by poison or malice;

8. extreme and repeated physical cruelty;

9. extreme and repeated mental cruelty;

10. conviction of a felony or other infamous crime; or,

11. infecting the other spouse with a sexually transmitted disease.

In a divorce case in which one spouse claims that the other party is guilty of one of the above fault grounds, that ground must be proven in order for the court to grant the divorce. In reality, this means that if you use one of the above fault reasons to file for divorce, make sure that you can prove it with evidence or witnesses. In other words, do not plead desertion if your spouse has never been absent. If you cannot prove one of these eleven, you probably should look at the grounds of irreconcilable differences.

Proving Fault Grounds   Remember, in order to allege that your spouse is at fault in a divorce, you must be able to present, in court, evidence of that fault. This cannot only be difficult, but it can be costly if you need to hire a group of private investigators to shadow your spouse. Another cost is the emotional turmoil on you in having to deal with the tangible evidence of what your spouse has done. If it is important to you that fault grounds be shown, you probably should retain an attorney to help you through this.

If you do decide to use fault grounds, the following are examples of what is usually used as evidence.

1. Unable to have sexual intercourse:

   - affidavit/testimony by either spouse detailing their lack of sexual intercourse;

   - medical records that prove inability; or,

   - affidavit/testimony by doctor.

2. Bigamy:

   - legal record of marriage from other state or

   - legal search of divorce records showing prior marriage was not dissolved.

3. Adultery:

   - pictures of spouse and paramour going into hotel;

   - pictures showing spouse having intimate relations with someone other than spouse; or,

   - records of spouse paying for trysts with someone other than spouse—usually hotel bills, travel accommodations, apartment payments.

4. Desertion:

   - legal documents and affidavits showing spouse was absent.

5. Drunkenness:

    - medical records;

    - police reports; or,

    - affidavits/testimony from doctors, witnesses, spouse.

6. Drugs:

    - medical records;

    - police reports; or,

    - affidavits/testimony from doctors, witnesses, spouse.

7. Attempt on life of spouse:

    - police reports or

    - affidavit/testimony from spouse or witnesses.

8. Physical cruelty:

    - pictures of injury;

    - medical and police reports; or,

    - affidavits/testimony from spouse and witnesses.

9. Mental cruelty:

    - medical reports or

    - affidavit/testimony from spouse and witnesses.

10. Conviction of crime:

    - police report and court records.

11. Sexually transmitted disease:

- medical reports or

- affidavit/testimony from spouse.

**Irreconcilable
Differences**

Illinois is technically not a *no-fault* state. This means that you still need to prove grounds in order to obtain a divorce. The ground that is the closest to no-fault is *irreconcilable differences*. With this ground, you tell the court, under oath, that:

> *irreconcilable differences have caused the irretrievable break-down of your marriage and that efforts at reconciliation have failed as would any future attempts at reconciliation which would be impracticable and not in the best interest of the family.*

While some people recite these words, you do not have to say these exact words. You do need to tell the court that the severe differences between you and your spouse have caused a breakdown of the marriage that can never be repaired, and that even trying to repair the marriage would not be the best thing for you or your family.

There is an additional requirement to using this ground. The parties must have lived:

- separate and apart for a continuous six months and both agree to this ground or

- separate and apart for a continuous two-year period.

The legal term *separate and apart* has been extended to include those spouses who live under the same roof but not as husband and wife. Some courts have found this to mean no physical contact between the two, freedom to come and go without explanation, funds kept separate, etc. Other courts look for separate bedrooms and no meaningful communication between the two, even though they can share finances.

CONTESTED

Divorce filed on both fault and no-fault grounds can be *contested* or *uncontested*. A *contested divorce* is one in which one spouse does not want the divorce and is willing to spend the time and money to fight the divorce, or issues that must be resolved through the divorce process cannot be agreed to. Contested divorces can go into multiple legal hearings and total up large legal fees. Technically, under the court system, once a complaint for a divorce is filed with the court, the divorce is considered as contested until all disputes are resolved.

You should attempt to resolve as many issues as possible before filing for a divorce so that your divorce is not contested. Contested divorces can drag out a bad situation to a point where a person has lost a significant amount of both time and money, only to be divorced in the end.

Contesting the actual divorce (not the splitting of property or issues regarding the children) often results in both spouses losing all their assets to pay for legal fees during years of contentious court battles. On the principle of refusing to agree to a divorce, spouses will spend every penny they have only to end up both divorced and broke.

For those who contest the divorce because they still are in love, the best thing to do is take the money you will invest in contesting this legal event and put it into professional counseling. You may be able to get your spouse to go with you to counseling if you offer to give him or her an uncontested divorce after a series of counseling sessions. Counseling can bring the spouses together or show you how to live on your own.

UNCONTESTED

Uncontested divorces are those in which all disputes have been resolved. Both parties have agreed on all matters, such as support, custody, visitation, and the division of marital property. Those with uncontested divorces are just waiting until the legal proceedings are done so that they can get on with their lives.

An uncontested divorce is really a good thing for the spouses, the children, and the other members of the family. The spouses have taken the time to discuss the pending divorce, and for whatever reason have decided to not spend the time and money fighting the inevitable family breakup. If you still do not want a divorce, remember—it will be easier to get back together if you have not put your spouse through the costs of a contested divorce.

Be warned that even though you and your spouse may agree on everything, the state of Illinois will not allow one attorney to represent *both* parties in a divorce action. Typically in such cases, one person is represented by the attorney and the other represents him- or herself (called *pro se*). However, this may not be the fairest situation for both parties. The party with the attorney may be able to take advantage of the person who represents him- or herself.

COLLABORATIVE DIVORCE

Collaborative divorce is a new term being used in divorces. A few lawyers in the country practice this process. It involves honest, cooperative work by both spouses and their attorneys to come up with a settlement in an uncontested divorce. There are several meetings between the parties and their attorneys along with a facilitator. It is very similar to mediation.

Along with collaborative divorce, some law firms are now offering divorce mediation for couples before filing for a divorce. This type of program will assist the parties in conflict resolution, which is done before going into court.

Not every case can or should go to these types of programs. It is up to the parties to decide if they could work things out with each other and if they need the assistance of a professional or will do it themselves.

DIVORCE MEDIATION

The term *mediation* can refer to two different things in a divorce. The first is a recent phenomenon that some law firms and independent companies are offering. A *professional mediator* assists the spouses in the creation of a *marital settlement agreement*. The mediator takes neither person's side and only facilitates the parties in coming to an agreement.

The second is covered in Illinois law. (750 ILCS 5/404.) Under this law, the court may require that the spouses take part in conciliation mediation or counseling. This can be ordered if the court concludes that there is a potential that the parties may *reconcile* (agree on differences). Many family law courts routinely order this as one last opportunity for the parties to stay married, especially if there are children involved. Sometimes a court will order this if one spouse requests it as a way to reconcile; however, this should not be used by one party as a way to stall the divorce process.

Many of the larger judicial districts have professional conciliation and counseling services as part of the judicial facility, while others use referrals. The notes and records of such conciliation and counseling sessions will not be used as part of the divorce record.

DIVORCE ARBITRATION

Arbitration is rarely used in divorce cases. *Arbitration* means that an arbitrator will listen to each side and make a decision, like a judge. Arbitration can be binding (you must do what the arbitrator says) or nonbinding (you can take the arbitrator's decision or not). Some long-running contested divorce cases may enlist an arbitrator to make certain decisions, usually about assets. In those cases, the arbitrator's decision is final and is adopted by the court.

The Divorce Process

The actual procedure for filing a divorce and the required documents vary from county to county. Generally, the first step is to file a Petition for Divorce (or *complaint*) with the court. You must also *serve* (deliver) a *Summons*, with a copy of the petition, on your spouse. The date you filed these items with the court is important, and will be used on all legal documents as the commencement date of the suit.

STEPS TO GETTING A DIVORCE

1. Make decisions. Decide the issues concerning grounds, custody, visitation, how you will divide the property and debts, and if there will there be spousal maintenance.

2. Fill out a Petition for Divorce.

3. File these forms with your Circuit Court clerk.

4. Notify your spouse that you have filed for divorce. Your spouse can then file a *Response* or *Answer* to your petition.

continued

5. Get a hearing date.

6. Prepare the forms needed at the hearing.

7. Attend the hearing.

8. Follow the judge's order.

See Chapter 8 for a detailed discussion of forms.

SUMMONS

A *Summons* is a legal notice to the person you are suing. In family law, it is used to notify your spouse that you are filing for a divorce, legal separation, annulment, custody, support, or an order of protection. You may also use a Praecipe for Summons in the case of divorces or legal separation when it is critical that the lawsuit be filed quickly, such as when your spouse is about to leave the jurisdiction of the Illinois court by moving overseas or to another state in an effort to avoid an Illinois divorce.

As with other lawsuits, it is usually the job of the sheriff's office or a private process service to deliver the Summons and complaint to your spouse. This must be done within a set time period from the date you file your complaint with the court. The time period that is allowed for serving or delivering the Summons is determined by each county court and will be printed on a *Service of Process* form, which you can obtain from your local county court.

NOTE: *The service of lawsuits is not restricted to the sheriff or professional process service. However, because a divorce can bring out the worst in spouses, it is highly recommended that you use one of these services. It is not unusual for those serving divorce papers to be the victim of a very angry spouse; even a spouse who expects the divorce can lash out. There is a fee for the sheriff or process server to serve the divorce papers.*

PETITION

If you and your spouse qualify for a *simplified dissolution of marriage*, the petition that you use is a form issued by the county. For all others, Illinois law lists what information is required on a Petition for Dissolution of Marriage. (750 ILCS 5/403.) This petition can be written by one of the spouses (called the *petitioner)* or by both spouses (called a *joint petition)*. Minimally, each petition should include:

- ✪ the name, age, occupation, address, and length of residence in Illinois of each party;

- ✪ the date of the marriage and where the marriage was registered;

- ✪ if another Dissolution of Marriage petition is pending in another state;

- ✪ that the parties are and have been residents of Illinois for more than ninety days, so they meet the jurisdictional requirements of the *Illinois Marriage and Dissolution Act*;

- ✪ that grounds for dissolution of the marriage do exist;

- ✪ names, ages, and addresses of all living children;

- ✪ if the wife is now pregnant;

- ✪ arrangements as to the support, custody, and visitation of the children;

- ✪ arrangements as to any spousal support; and,

- ✪ the relief asked for (dissolution of marriage, approval of Marital Settlement Agreement if one is submitted, or approval of Joint Parenting Agreement is one is submitted).

This information is the minimum required by the state for this petition. Most petitions contain much more. Every Dissolution of Marriage Petition is as unique as the parties. This is a legal document that is created new for each married couple who wishes to divorce.

One example of an additional item that may be included in a dissolution petition is covered in Illinois Statutes. (750 ILCS 5/413.) A woman can request that her former (maiden) name be restored in a divorce petition. If she is considering returning to her former last name, this is the best place to do it. Otherwise, she may be required to initiate another court proceeding and pay additional fees to change names.

There are a few items that are the same on every dissolution petition. Centered and in capital letters at the top of the page is the court identification. This is usually "IN THE CIRCUIT COURT OF _____." Next, there are two or three blank lines. Then the page is divided by a vertical line. On the left side are the names of the parties and their legal titles (*petitioner* or *respondent*). The right side of the line is left blank for the court-assigned *case number*. The names of the parties are *petitioner* (the one who brought the suit) first and then the name of the *respondent* (the one being sued) second. An example of how this should look follows.

STATE OF ILLINOIS
IN THE CIRCUIT COURT OF THE [number of circuit] **JUDICIAL CIRCUIT OF** [name of county] **COUNTY**

IN RE THE MARRIAGE OF:)
)
[your name]   )
)
       Petitioner   )
)
  and   )
)
[your spouse's name]   )
)
     Respondent   )

[Title of Form]

APPEARANCE AND AGREEMENT

If you and your spouse did not agree to a joint petition, once your spouse receives these documents, he or she is required to file an Appearance and a written response with the court. The Appearance is merely a form that your spouse fills out and files with the court. Your spouse's response will determine what happens next.

There are several options as to the next step in a divorce. If both parties agree to the divorce, you and your spouse may begin working on a Joint Marital Settlement Agreement (see Chapter 11) or a Joint Parenting Agreement (see Chapter 14) to submit to the court with or without the assistance of an attorney. If your spouse does not want a divorce, he or she may begin a fight that may end up in a trial.

RESPONSE TO YOUR PETITION

Once your spouse has been served with your Petition for Divorce, he or she must respond to the court. This *Response* or *Answer* can take different forms. For some, this is just an opportunity to lash out in writing. For others, it is time to put some very embarrassing things in writing. Do not let this response surprise you—it does not surprise the court.

Most courts are used to couples fighting by making allegations in writing during a divorce. Your spouse will be required to support those allegations in front of a judge, just as you support your fault grounds with evidence. If the responses or answers from your spouse include allegations, you should obtain an attorney to assist you in what will probably be a very contentious divorce proceeding.

DIVORCE TRIAL

The first step in a divorce that is headed for trial is to file pretrial orders, which attempt to resolve disputes such as living arrangements, custody, support, and visitation. These pretrial orders may result in *temporary orders* from the court directing support, custody, visitation, or other matters.

The next step is the discovery process. This process is where each side obtains information on the marriage, the other spouse, and other issues that effect the divorce. *Depositions* (recorded question and answer sessions) may be taken of each spouse and their witnesses. Negotiations may then begin to resolve the contested issues. If the spouses cooperate and resolve their differences, a Marital Settlement Agreement will be drafted, signed by each spouse, and presented to the court. The court will approve the divorce on the terms listed in this agreement. If the spouses still cannot resolve their differences, then the court will proceed to a series of hearings, the last one called a *pretrial hearing*, to set the trial date. A divorce trial is run just like any other trial. The attorneys speak to the court, witnesses testify under oath, and the judge makes a ruling.

Of course, this type of trial can become very expensive and time-consuming. In the end, those unresolved differences will be resolved by the court and the resolution may be something that neither spouse wanted.

DISCLOSURE STATEMENTS

Many counties in Illinois are now requiring the filing of a *Financial Disclosure Statement* or an *Asset Disclosure Statement* from each party to a divorce.

NOTE: *Financial Disclosure Statement and Asset Disclosure Statement are two different names for the same thing.*

This financial information is filled in on forms from the county, and each party must swear that the information is true. Besides filing these forms with the court, the other spouse must, by law, get a copy of them. The primary use is for the court to determine support, maintenance, and division of property.

SIMPLIFIED DIVORCE

Illinois has several laws for those who qualify for a simplified divorce. (750 ILCS 5/451 through 5/467.) In order to qualify to use this procedure, you and your spouse must meet *all* of the following conditions.

☉   Neither party is dependent on the other for support or the dependent party is willing to sign away his or her right to support.

☉   Either party meets the residency requirement of living ninety days in Illinois and considers Illinois as his or her domicile.

☉   Irreconcilable differences have caused the irretrievable breakdown of the marriage, the parties have lived apart for six months or more, efforts at reconciliation have failed, and future attempts would be impracticable and not in the best interest of the family.

☉   No children were born or adopted of this marriage and the wife is not pregnant now.

☉   The marriage did not exceed eight years.

☉   Neither party has any interest in *real property* (real estate, land).

☉   The total fair market value of all marital property is less than $10,000, the combined gross annual income from all sources is less than $35,000, and neither party has a gross annual income greater than $20,000.

☉   The parties have disclosed all assets and tax returns for the years married to each other.

☉   The parties have executed a written agreement that divides all assets that are valued at more than $100 and divides responsibilities for paying outstanding debts between them.

If both parties qualify, they will fill the **JOINT PETITION FOR SIMPLIFIED DISSOLUTION OF MARRIAGE** forms with the court. (See Appendix D for a generic copy of this form.) Some counties have a brochure that describes how to file for a simplified divorce in that county. Call the office of the clerk of the Circuit Court in your county to see if one is available. (see Appendix A.)

NOTE: *The simplified dissolution forms are self-explanatory and have instructions on the form.*

Both parties will be required to appear in court and to swear that all submitted information is accurate. Normally, the judge will question both parties as to their agreement to divide both the assets and the debts of the marriage. Both parties will be required to submit a statement, called an *affidavit*, in which they swear under oath that the property has been divided in accordance with the agreement that was submitted to the court.

Divorce Forms

In this book and on any Internet site that talks about divorce, you will notice that this legal action is a sea of forms. Divorce forms can be confusing even to attorneys. This chapter attempts to make some sense out of forms you will need and those you may need, how to get the right forms for your court, and how to prepare forms.

IN GENERAL—CIRCUIT COURTS

Before you start filling out the forms, you should know something about how divorce forms got so complex. Each Circuit Court has a different title and a different clerk, whose name must appear on court forms. Depending on the population, a Circuit Court within a county can have several judges who may want to track different information on divorce forms in their court. Additionally, laws change and more information is required. That is why each circuit has different forms and how the forms became complex.

How does that affect a person who wants to file his or her own divorce? First, know that Illinois courts strongly encourage people to retain attorneys for the divorce procedure in order to protect the parties who are divorcing. This is one of the most stressful times of your life and it is easy, when under stress, to make bad mistakes. Unfortunately, mistakes made during the divorce process can cause you problems for the rest of your life.

For this reason, many Circuit Courts concentrate on the *Simplified Dissolution of Marriage* forms package when providing detailed instructions for filling out the complex divorce forms. This simplified dissolution, as discussed in Chapter 7, has very limiting restrictions and requirements as to which couples can use this type of form. For the majority of couples, the simplified dissolution will not work. If you are part of this majority and still want to do your own divorce filing, you will be stuck with the myriad of complex court forms.

The second thing to know about filing your own forms is that you *must* use the proper form for each Circuit Court. This is a non-negotiable requirement. The goal with forms is to have the correct forms filled in properly so that there is no delay or question when it comes to filing for a divorce.

FORMS ON THE INTERNET

For years, attorneys who practiced divorce law in several circuits needed to keep a stock of up-to-date paper forms for each circuit and each judge within the circuit. Now many of the Circuit Court are available on the Internet. In Appendix A, you will see that a number of circuit clerks now have websites, and the majority of these websites allow you to download forms from the Internet. Using these websites gives you the most current version of the form prepared before attempting to file it in court.

Remember, if you want to file your own case you must use the correct form for the court you are filing in and the correct form for the action you want to achieve. For the majority of Illinois citizens, this means you can either download the right forms from the circuit clerk's site in your county or go over to the courthouse for the right forms.

COURT FILING

A court keeps a file on each suit filed. This is a real file with papers in an expandable folder or attached at the top to a thick paper folder. Each file is given a number, called the *case number*. It is used to keep track of the case, and in most courthouses, is the way cases are organized. Filing a document with the court is a way to make a record of an event or statement, give notice that you are planning to sue, or respond to a current suit.

The act of filing a document means that you have prepared all the required forms, you have made the number of copies required by your court, and you take these copies to the circuit clerk. The circuit clerk will stamp the copies with a date stamp that shows the date you filed the document and will charge you a fee for filing. The number of copies required and the amount of money charged as a fee depends on the type of document and the court. You will probably need to call the circuit clerk to ask about these issues. (See Appendix A for phone numbers of Circuit Courts.)

Most times, the clerk will not check to see that your documents are filled out right or are the correct ones to use. If you mention that you are a *pro se* (the legal term for representing yourself), you may be able to get some assistance. In some of the larger counties, there are legal assistance volunteers who are in the courthouse to help pro se people.

Once a suit is filed with the court, you will be given other tasks to complete. You may be required to file other documents and appear at a hearing. If you are required to file other documents, you will be given a date to file these. You must do that on time. If you fail to file something on time, you can lose your case and may be required to pay additional fees to start over.

COMMON FORMS

While each Circuit Court can require certain forms be used in obtaining a divorce, there are a handful of common forms that are used in most divorce cases. The form may look different from one court to another, but the reason for the form is usually the same.

The most common forms used in a divorce are as follows.

- ✪ *Appearance Form.* An appearance form tells the court who you are and that you are representing yourself in this case. Not all courts require this form for pro se litigants. If the court requires this form, you would submit it when you file the very first forms.

- ✪ *Application to Proceed as a Poor Person.* Use this to obtain legal assistance from the courts. Not everyone will qualify for free or low-cost legal assistance this way. You may want to contact private legal assistance providers. Also, many bar associations and law schools have their own low-cost legal assistance programs.

- ✪ *Summons.* This form is used to notify the person you are suing. There is a wide variety in the format used to indicate a summons. In some courts, this is a separate document that is prepared by the person who is suing; in others, it is a small sheet that the sheriff who serves the summons attaches to the legal document. In a divorce, the summons is attached to the Petition for Dissolution of Marriage. That package is served on the other spouse, and is his or her legal notification that a divorce is pending.

- ✪ *Petition for Dissolution of Marriage.* This form is usually tailored to the couple's situation. There are differences when the couple has children, when the couple files jointly, and when one spouse files against the other. Of course, that tailoring is in addition to the specifics added by each Circuit Court. This form must be filed to begin the divorce proceeding.

- ✪ *Affidavit in Response.* When one spouse sues the other for divorce (as opposed to filing a Joint Petition for Divorce), the spouse being sued may use this form. The person who initiated the divorce normally uses this form when the spouse being sued for divorce wants maintenance, child support, custody, or payment of other fees.

✪ *Judgment for Dissolution of Marriage.* This form goes hand-in-hand with the petition. It is tailored to the couple's situation and the decisions made by the court.

You will need to get the correct forms from your local Circuit Court.

GENERIC FORMS

Not every circuit clerk provides these forms. If they have not prepared blank forms for you to use, you can go and ask to see another divorce file and tailor your form to match what someone else has filed, or you can use the generic forms provided here. These can be used when your Circuit Court does not have forms on the Internet. There is no guarantee that the court will allow you to file these. You may need to rewrite the information on one of the approved forms right at the courthouse, but this gives you an approximation of what information you will need.

Remember, in order to have the proper form, you should download the form from the Circuit Court's website or get the form at the courthouse. If all this sounds confusing, it is, which is why divorcing couples are urged to turn their divorce over to an attorney.

Appendix D provides you with a generic version of the most commonly used forms in a divorce. The following section will explain the purpose of each form and how to fill each one out.

Caption (form 1)
The way to make any form work for your Circuit Court is to change the **CAPTION**. (see p.58.) Using Appendix A, you should put the number of the Circuit Court and the name of the county in the **CAPTION** to make a form work for your Circuit Court. Form 1 is a generic **CAPTION** that must be at the top of every form submitted to the court. Complete the **CAPTION** as follows.

⬦ Using Appendix A, enter the number of the Circuit Court in the second line.

⬦ Using Appendix A, enter the name of the county you live in on the third line.

➢ Put your name just before the word "Petitioner."

➢ Put your spouse's name just before the word "Respondent."

➢ On the next line, include the title for the form you are creating.

> **NOTE:** *Even attorneys sometimes have problems deciding what title to put on a form. Look at one of the websites suggested in Appendix A. Specifically, look at how the forms are titled. That way, you can pick a title that is close to what you need.*

Application to Proceed as a Poor Person (form 2)

The **APPLICATION TO PROCEED AS A POOR PERSON** (form 2) is a request that the court determine you are a poor person, and provide you with legal assistance. Use the following instructions to fill out form 2.

➢ Enter the number of the Circuit Court, the name of the county, your name, and your spouse's name, as instructed in form 1.

➢ "No." is the case number assigned by the clerk to your case.

➢ Under the title, enter your name and age (age at the time you are filling this form out).

➢ In #2, list your occupation and where you get income from. This can be a job, public aid, or assistance from other people.

➢ In #3, write how much money you made last year. If you do not know, estimate.

➢ In #4, write how much money you expect to make this year. Again, you can estimate if you are not sure.

➢ For #5, list all the people who you support and their ages. This is not limited to just people the courts have ordered you to support legally. Include everyone you provide financial support for.

➢ In this section, list your assets. If you have real estate (a home or property), write the address here. List the personal property you own, including things such as cars, motorcycles, boats, televisions, furniture, or anything of value.

◈ Read the last paragraph and sign on the line provided.

◈ Record the date that you signed this document on the line provided.

Petition for Order of Protection (form 3)

The PETITION FOR ORDER OF PROTECTION is used to apply for a court Order of Protection. Before you begin filling out this form, review Chapter 5 on Protection. Complete form 3 as follows.

◈ Enter the number of the Circuit Court, the name of the county, your name, and the name of the person you are getting an order of protection against as instructed in form 1.

◈ "No." is the case number assigned by the clerk to your case.

◈ Select the type of protection you want. Again, review Chapter 5 for an explanation of the types of protection.

◈ Under "Petitioner's Information," fill in your name, current address, date of birth, Social Security number, and sex.

◈ Under "Respondent's Information," fill in information on the person you are getting the Order of Protection against: his or her name, current address, date of birth, Social Security number, sex, race, height, weight, color of hair, color of eyes, and work address.

NOTE: *The reason for the extra details is that law enforcement officers need to be able to spot this person by sight.*

◈ Answer "yes" or "no" for the following questions about the person you are getting the Order of Protection against.

• Is this person a police officer?

• Does this person usually carry a weapon?

• Do you consider this person dangerous?

• Do you believe this person may take his or her own life?

◈ Enter the relationship between you and the person you are getting this order against.

◈ Answer if this order is to protect you or your children.

◈ Explain (in your own words) why you want the Order of Protection. It is common to list if you or your children were threatened by this person.

◈ Under "Remedies," state what you want the court to do. This can be as simple as, "keep [this person] away from my children and me."

◈ Sign the document and enter the date you signed.

Stipulation (form 4)

The STIPULATION (form 4) is used if you are filing for a *no-fault* divorce, to waive that two-year period of living apart in order to get a faster divorce. Fill out form 4 using the following directions.

◈ Enter the number of the Circuit Court, the name of the county, your name, and your spouse's name as instructed in form 1.

◈ "No." is the case number assigned by the clerk to your case.

◈ After the words "NOW COME," fill in your name and your spouse's name as on the caption.

◈ Enter the number of months you and your spouse have lived apart.

◈ You and your spouse will need to *both* sign this document in front of a notary public.

Joint Petition for Simplified Dissolution of Marriage (form 5)

The JOINT PETITION FOR SIMPLIFIED DISSOLUTION OF MARRIAGE is the first document filed with the court in order to begin the divorce. Complete form 5 as follows.

◈ Enter the number of the Circuit Court, the name of the county, your name, and your spouse's name as instructed in form 1.

◈ "No." is the case number assigned by the clerk to your case.

◈ On the first line, fill in your name.

◈ On the second line, fill in your spouse's name.

◈ #1—this is information about you. Your current age, your occupation, and where you currently live. Cross out the word "HAS" or "HAS NOT" to indicate if you have lived in Illinois for the past ninety days.

◈ #2—this is information about your spouse. Your spouse's current age, occupation, and where he or she currently live. Cross out the word "HAS" or "HAS NOT" to indicate if you have lived in Illinois for the past ninety days.

◈ #3—enter the date of the marriage, the county you were married in, and the state where you were married.

◈ #4—read this section. If there were no children of this marriage and the wife is not now pregnant, enter the name of the wife.

◈ #5—read this section. If the statements are true, enter the date that the parties began to live separately.

◈ Read sections #6, #7, and #8.

◈ Read #9 and enter the gross income of both you and your spouse.

◈ Read #10.

◈ If the wife wishes to return to her former name, fill in the wife's current name, and the name the wife wishes to return to.

◈ Both you and your spouse need to sign at the bottom of the document and enter the date that this document was signed.

CHECKLISTS AND WORKSHEETS

Before preparing any of the paper forms, look at Appendix C. Appendix C contains ten worksheets for your use in deciding to divorce. These forms will help you organize your information, keep track of your assets, determine child support amounts, and give you a picture of what needs to be addressed in a divorce.

If you use the assistance of an attorney, he or she will probably require all this information and more. You may be able to cut down your time in the lawyer's office by having your information organized before you go to the office. If you and your spouse are working out a settlement, these worksheets can help you get your financial needs in order and may get you to an agreement faster.

Make copies of these worksheets, modify them for your needs, and use them as another tool in your divorce.

Marital Property

Other than issues dealing with children, the next biggest area for dispute in a divorce is anything that has to do with what each spouse will get out of the marriage. From dividing up the property that the couple has accumulated during their marriage to spousal support, a couple in a contentious divorce can spend an enormous amount of time (and legal fees) just fighting about these items. Before you begin the process of dividing up your things, it is a good idea to know what is considered marital property and is therefore subject to being shared with your spouse.

MARITAL PROPERTY

Any discussion about divorce will use the term *marital property*. Courts make the determination as to what is marital property and then divide that property up between the spouses by the guidelines in the law. Marital property is defined in the Illinois statutes as *all the property that is acquired by either spouse **during** the marriage.* (750 ILCS 5/503.)

There is some property that is not considered marital property, such as:

- ✪ property that is given to one spouse as a gift or through a will;

- ✪ property that is acquired before the marriage;

- ✪ property that is received in exchange for the two above examples;

- ✪ property obtained after a legal separation;

- ✪ property that is excluded by a valid legal agreement or court judgment from being considered marital property; and,

- ✪ income from an increase in value of any property listed above.

If the spouses own property in a state in which all property (marital or other) is divided 50/50, then the Illinois court will consider it as owned 50/50 by each spouse. Furthermore, all pension benefits acquired by either spouse during the marriage are considered marital property. (A *Qualified Illinois Domestic Relation Order* will be needed to divide these pension benefits. If you are in this situation, you need an attorney.) Finally, when marital and nonmarital property are mixed to the point that the nonmarital property can no longer be identified, then the property is considered all marital. Examples of this are shares of stock, nonmarital money used to purchase marital property, and other commodities investments.

Courts consider any financial verdicts or settlements from personal injury lawsuits that were filed during the marriage as marital property. There have also been decisions in which the court rules that the royalties from performances or books that were created during the marriage are marital property, even if those royalties come years after the marriage was dissolved.

If one spouse expends a personal effort to contribute to the value of nonmarital property, usually in the case of inherited property that needs repair before selling, then that contribution is considered marital property. The courts look at how much the personal effort increased the value of the item and then assign a value to that contribution.

Make a list of the property in your home. Go from the home, the cars, and the furniture, down to the dishes and pans. You can use Worksheet 6 in Appendix C or simply a lined pad. Write down the asset and next to it which spouse gets that asset. You will then see what items you need to negotiate on.

Be smart. Do not hold up a divorce over a two dollar cream pitcher, even it is your favorite. There are many cases in which spouses fight over the smallest things, to the point where they have spent more in legal fees than the item is worth. Besides, if you leave it up to the court to make a decision you have a 50/50 chance of losing. Negotiate with your spouse on these things, and remember, negotiation means that both people have to give a little.

RULES OF THUMB ON MARITAL ASSETS

1. Personal property purchased with money earned by either spouse during the marriage is marital property (owned by both).

2. Personal property owned by one spouse before marriage remains the property of that spouse only.

3. Property given to a spouse individually (even gifts from the other spouse) is the property of that spouse only.

4. Property given to the couple as a family (gifts from parents) during the marriage is marital property (owned by both).

5. Property purchased by one spouse after the couple has separated in anticipation of divorce or legal separation is the property of that spouse only.

Unusual Assets

Next to who gets the marital home, the second thing most often litigated in a divorce is who gets the pets. In many marriages, these pets are the *children* and both spouses will fight to the death to protect their *furry children*. If this is you, select an attorney who understands the attachment of people to their pets. Many enterprising attorneys have drawn up something similar to a child custody agreement with a visitation schedule for pets. It can be done and courts will recognize it.

Factors   In determining questions of what is marital property, courts consider:

- ❂   contribution of both spouses;

- ❂   the use of the item by both;

- ❂   the value each spouse has assigned to the item;

- ❂   the length of marriage;

- ❂   the economic circumstances of each spouse;

- ❂   obligations from prior marriages;

- ❂   any prenuptial agreements; and,

- ❂   the best interests of the children.

The Marital Home   The female spouse does not always get the marital home. Actually, courts look at several factors when deciding who gets this major asset. Things that the courts look at when making this decision are:

- ❂   the amount of equity in the home;

- ❂   ability of each spouse to afford the utilities and other home costs;

- ❂   the amount of assets awarded to each spouse;

- ❂   the income of each spouse;

- ❂   the length of the marriage;

- ❂   the length of time each person lived in this house;

- ❂   the best interests of the children; and,

- ❂   the reasons each spouse gives for wanting the home.

Of course, if the couple decides prior to going into court who gets the house, the court will most likely allow that decision to stand. The only time a court would disturb that decision is when the best interest of the children may be affected.

The *best interest* of the children is one of the major factors a court uses when determining what is marital property. This is what leads to courts awarding the entire marital home to the person who gets custody of the children, ignoring the rules of marital property. This type of decision usually comes with a requirement that after the children have reached majority or are out of school, the marital property is divided as per the statutes. Courts will usually attempt to keep minor children in their marital home despite the spouse's desire to sell the property.

A common resolution for the marital home is to allow the custodial parent to live in the home with the children. Both spouses then split the expenses of the home either on a 50/50 basis or by a percentage calculation. Once the children are beyond age 18, then the spouses sell the home and split the profits.

Another variation on that schedule is to allow one of the spouses to pay the other spouse 50% of the value of the home and buy out the other spouse. Some spouses agree to complicated calculations to keep their home. It is not unusual for a spouse to waive receiving maintenance in order to have sole ownership of the martial home.

– Warning –

People who attempt to transfer marital property to a third party in an attempt to keep that property from the other spouse can be found in *contempt of court*. Family law judges are keenly aware of attempts to defraud the other spouse and do not tolerate this action.

If you allow the court to determine what is marital property and how it should be divided up, you will surely be disappointed. You can avoid the court's interference by determining what property goes to each spouse in a Marital Settlement Agreement. (see Chapter 11.)

Maintenance

Spousal support or *maintenance* is another aspect that needs to be understood before you begin the divorce process. Courts are unlikely to award maintenance, and if they do, they usually make it only temporary. A woman, for example, can no longer rely on getting any spousal support—even if she gets custody of the children—in a divorce.

MAINTENANCE, SPOUSAL SUPPORT, OR ALIMONY

Maintenance, *spousal support*, or *alimony* all mean the same thing. It is an amount of money paid by one spouse to another either on a temporary or permanent basis. Illinois uses the term "maintenance," and will award maintenance in a divorce or legal separation. Maintenance is awarded by agreement of the parties or at the direction of the court without regard to misconduct. It is strictly an economic decision.

Temporary maintenance is for a specific time—a particular date or until a particular occurrence. *Permanent maintenance* is lifetime support and is rarely awarded, even in situations in which a spouse has no job. Courts look at a spouse's ability to support him- or herself, not the current job. The sad statistics are that after a divorce, the financial standard of living for the majority of women drops 25% to 50%, while the financial standard of living for the man significantly increases.

Illinois does not give any guidance as to what the normal duration of maintenance should be. Usually, the temporary maintenance ends when the court believes that the person receiving maintenance can make his or her own financial way, but this is a subjective term. One way to handle this is for the couple to agree to maintenance until the spouse earns a certain level of income.

The Law   Illinois law gives very little direction as to when maintenance is required or how to calculate maintenance. While the court says that it will make every effort to award maintenance in a spirit of equity and fairness, some cases do not seem to fit that. In a recent case, the court stated that it was not required to equalize the net income of both spouses. (*In re Marriage of Reynard*, 344 Ill.App.3d 785, 801 N.E.2d 591, 279 Ill.Dec. 917 (4th Dist. 2004).)In another case, the court awarded the 66-year-old wife 84% of all the marital assets but no maintenance. The court stated that this was equitable because the 69-year-old husband kept his entire pension. (*In re Marriage of Gaumer*, 2003 Il. App. LEXIS 94 (5th Dist. 2003).) Finally, in yet another case, the court found that a maintenance award should be fashioned on the basis of all the circumstances disclosed. This includes a person's pension payments and social security benefits. (*In re Marriage of Rogers*, No. 4-04-0003 (released Oct. 14, 2004).)

Illinois statutes address the issue of maintenance. (750 ILCS 5/504.) This law lists twelve factors that the court must consider in the award of maintenance. The only direction the law gives are the twelve factors that courts must use to determine maintenance, which are:

1. income and property of each party;

2. needs of each party;

3. present and future earning capacity of each party;

4. any impairment to earning capacity;

5. time needed to get appropriate training and education for employment;

6. standard of living during the marriage;

7. duration of the marriage;

8. age, and physical and emotional health of each party;

9. tax consequences;

10. contributions and services by each party to the other's license, education, or training during the marriage;

11. agreements between parties; and,

12. any other fact that the court finds to be just and equitable.

In the case *Re Marriage of Klein*, the court considered that the spouse receiving maintenance was cohabiting with her boyfriend and denied her request for maintenance due to the boyfriend's financial support. (231 Ill.App.3d 901, 596 N.E.2d 1214, 173 Ill.Dec. 335 (4th Dist. 1992).)

Rehabilitation by Maintenance

Courts now look at maintenance as a means of rehabilitation for one spouse, so that spouse can be financially independent. This is a move towards spousal self-sufficiency and the elimination of support dependency. Courts can require that one spouse get the training and education that is needed in order to become self-sufficient. During this training time, the spouse will receive temporary maintenance. If the court does order this type of rehabilitation, the spouse being trained will be required to periodically report to the court under oath so that the duration of maintenance will not be abused.

Self-sufficiency. Courts take the issue of self-sufficiency so seriously that there have been cases in which those who had previously received permanent maintenance were required to work toward becoming self-sufficient. This seems to be the case when there is a temporary disability, a health problem that is cured, or a change of careers. In these cases, Illinois courts have carved out an *affirmative obligation* (required steps) of the person who received maintenance to get training or skills to become self-sufficient.

Permanent Maintenance. Courts are required to give consideration for permanent maintenance for those who gave up their career to be a stay-at-home parent. However, in reality, unless that spouse is aged or disabled, most courts will require that they, too, work toward being self-sufficient. An aged, unemployed spouse who cannot work should not only request permanent maintenance, but a permanent continuation of health care insurance as well.

TERMINATING AND CHANGING MAINTENANCE

Life changes and so do the orders of maintenance. That husband making seven figures may find himself out of a job, or the wife studying for a degree suddenly finds herself disabled. Things happen and the law allows an adjustment to maintenance orders accordingly, but there must be a *substantial change in circumstances*. The court is directed by law to review these changes in light of the following factors:

- ✪ good faith changes in employment (you cannot quit your job to avoid paying maintenance);

- ✪ the spouse receiving maintenance had made reasonable efforts to become self-supporting;

- ✪ there is real impairment in the present and future capacity of the spouse receiving maintenance;

- ✪ the tax consequences of maintenance;

- ✪ how long maintenance has been paid to how long the marriage was;

- ✪ the property awarded to the spouse in the divorce;

✪   the change in both spouses' income since the divorce;

✪   the property acquired since the divorce; and,

✪   any other factor that the court expressly finds to be just and equitable. (750 ILCS 5/510 (a-5).)

Settlement Agreement

The Marital Settlement Agreement is the heart of a divorce decree. (see Appendix E.) It contains all the details as to separation of property, and if there are children, it will also contain details as to anything that deals with the children. Those who intend to divorce will end up with a settlement agreement whether they cooperate at the beginning of the divorce process or go through years of divorce bickering. Even those spouses who enter into several actual trials to get a divorce will end up with some type of settlement agreement, either written by the spouses or by the court.

Logically, since the parties will eventually end up with such an agreement, it would seem that both parties would cooperate in drafting this agreement. If the divorcing spouses would cooperate to negotiate this agreement themselves early in the divorce proceedings, it would save both time and money. Unfortunately, what usually happens is the warring spouses get their separate attorneys to fight over each item. After the divorce, the warring spouses may find themselves with legal bills that are many times the cost of the stuff they fought so hard for.

MARITAL SETTLEMENT AGREEMENTS

Drawing up a Marital Settlement Agreement is the best thing that a husband and wife can do to protect themselves during divorce. There are many benefits for having this agreement. It allows the parties to divide up their property as they see fit. If it includes a Joint Parenting Agreement, it gives the parties the ability to set up visitation schedules and some child support expenses that are agreeable to each spouse (subject to court approval). It saves the money that would be spent on attorneys doing the same negotiations at an hourly rate. It forces both spouses to work together, which is something they must do for a long time if there are minor children in the marriage.

A Marital Settlement Agreement is a legal contract between both spouses. This agreement can include anything that the two spouses want. It details how all marital property is being divided between the spouses, both the assets and the debts. If real estate is involved, it can include dates of the transfer of the deed or a copy of a deed that does such a transfer. Maintenance payments should be detailed, and if this is *rehabilitative maintenance* (support for a limited time), the date or the occurrence when it ends should be included.

A Marital Settlement Agreement can include anything. The following is a suggestion as to how to set up your agreement and what it should include.

1. Basics:

    • names and addresses of parties;

    • date of agreement;

    • date married and where;

    • names of children and their birth dates;

    • names of each party's attorney; and,

    • a statement that this agreement was made freely by both parties, that this document is the entire agreement, and that the agreement was not done to stimulate divorce.

settlement agreement   87

2.   Spousal support or maintenance information in detail.

3.   Division of property in detail.

4.   Joint parental agreement:

    • custody;

    • visitation; and,

    • support.

5.   Signatures of both parties.

If there are children, there should be a Joint Parenting Agreement that details:

❂   child support payments (when payments are due);

❂   what happens if the payments stop;

❂   who will provide the children's health care;

❂   the visitation schedule;

❂   where the children will spend holidays; and,

❂   various other items that deal with the children.

The family law court will review only that part of this agreement that deals with the children to make sure that it complies with the law and is in the best interest of the children.

HOW COURTS VIEW MARITAL SETTLEMENT AGREEMENTS

Usually, judges will allow the parties to make their own Marital Settlement Agreements without any interference. This is how the law puts it:

The terms of the agreement, except those providing for the support, custody and visitation of children, are binding upon the court unless it finds, after considering the economic circumstances of the parties and any other relevant evidence produced by the parties, on their own motion or on request of the court, that the agreement is unconscionable. (750 ILCS 5/502 (b).)

What this means is that anything in your agreement that deals with children will be scrutinized, but the rest of it will probably be accepted unless one of the spouses objects or the judge feels that the agreement is way out of line.

Unconscionable, in legal terms, is a bargain that is so one-sided that no one would accept unless forced. Once a judge finds a Marital Settlement Agreement unconscionable, he or she can reject the entire thing, make the parties submit a revised agreement, or divide the property up as he or she sees fit. More and more judges are reading the sections dealing with children in a settlement agreement and making judgment upon the contents. However, do not trust that a judge will notice mere unfairness. Many times, what is unfair to a certain person just does not rise to the level of being unconscionable. Do not sign something you feel is unfair—continue to negotiate until you can wholeheartedly agree to the terms of the settlement.

Do not write or agree to an unconscionable settlement. If you and your spouse decide to make an agreement—and you should in order to save time and money—keep it fair. Fair is when both sides give a little and both sides get a little.

OTHER AGREEMENTS THAT WILL AFFECT A DIVORCE

Besides the Marital Settlement Agreement there are two other agreements that may limit the amount of property or amount of maintenance that a spouse can get upon divorce. Like the Marital Settlement Agreement, these two agreements can also contain any other items that the couple wants to include, within reason.

Premarital or Antenuptial Agreement

An agreement that the couple signs prior to getting married is called a *premarital* or *antenuptial agreement*. At one time only the rich used this, but it has become more common as more women are entering into the work force and purchasing their own property. It is also a very good tool for those parents who are entering into a new marriage in order to financially protect their children from a prior marriage.

In Illinois, premarital agreements are governed by *Illinois Uniform Premarital Agreement Act*. (750 ILCS 10/1 et seq.) Basically, the agreement must be in writing and signed by both parties. By law, a premarital agreement can define the rights and obligations of each party as to:

- property (both marital and nonmarital);

- spousal support;

- wills or trusts;

- death benefits; or,

- any other matter except child support.

The agreement goes into effect when the couple become validly married and usually will only be enforced upon death of one spouse or upon divorce.

Not enforced. If you and your spouse entered into a premarital agreement, it probably will have an effect on what you receive upon a divorce. Review the terms of the premarital agreement prior to negotiating the Marital Settlement Agreement. You may find that certain property has already been negotiated away or that you have more than you expect. If you hire an attorney to handle your divorce, bring your premarital agreement to your attorney so he or she can review it.

Illinois is very specific about the reasons that such an agreement would not be enforced. If one of the parties was forced into signing the agreement, if one of the parties did not fully disclose their property or financial obligations to the other, or if the agreement is considered unconscionable, then courts will not enforce the agreement.

Postnuptial Agreement

A *postnuptial agreement* is a rarely used type of contract made between a husband and wife. This type of contract can be used to define the rights and obligations of an existing spouse, just as the pre-marital agreement does. The most common instance of this agreement being used is when one spouse comes into a large amount of money, such as a lottery winning, and does not want his or her spouse to take half that money in a divorce.

Some courts have found that this type of contract is an attempt to financially force a spouse to stay married, and they still gave the divorcing spouse a portion of the money. Before you enter into this type of contract, you probably need to consult an attorney. Like a pre-marital agreement, this agreement can affect what you receive upon a divorce. If you hire an attorney to handle your divorce, bring any postnuptial agreements to your attorney to review.

Children
and Divorce

chapter 12

Children and their emotional well-being should be the primary focus of parents getting a divorce. Parents who divorce will be required to put aside their personal differences in order to raise their children. This chapter focuses on general topics.

BEST INTEREST OF THE CHILD

Any discussion of children in a divorce situation refers to a law called the *best interest of the child*. In Illinois, this is written in the statutes. (750 ILCS 5/602.) This law requires that the court look at the best interest of the child in custody determinations. Since this law was passed, court cases have expanded this so that all decisions that effect the children in a divorce are made after determining what is in the best interest of the children.

This law states that the court shall consider the following factors in determining custody:

- ✪ the wishes of the child's parents;

- ✪ the wishes of the child;

- the interaction and interrelationship of the child with parents, siblings, friends, relatives, teachers, and others of significance;

- the child's adjustment to his or her home, school, and community;

- mental and physical health of all involved;

- physical violence or threat of physical violence by the potential custodian toward the child and others;

- occurrence of ongoing domestic violence; and,

- the willingness and ability of each parent to facilitate and encourage a close and continuing relationship between the minor child and the other parent.

EMOTIONS

Two people who no longer want to be married can blame each other and cause damage to each other's psychological well-being. As a society, we accept such actions from those who are splitting up. The problem comes when this split up affects the children in the relationship. Children are raised to love both of their parents. The parents are providers, role models, the givers of love. So what happens when these same parents decide to divorce? In many cases, the children are forgotten or even used as pawns to hurt the other spouse.

If you are planning to divorce, tell your children. Explain a divorce in age-appropriate terms. *Do not* blame the children for the breakup. *Do not* get the children to spy on your ex-spouse. *Do not* make the children take sides. *Do not* use your children as your emotional sounding board.

No matter how hard it is, never talk badly of their other parent. If you need to vent about your ex-spouse, call a friend or a professional counselor. While your rage may well be justified, it should not be opened up to your children. Children need to be supported during a divorce. They need the unconditional love of both parents and the reassurance that they did not cause the divorce.

CHILDREN'S BILL OF RIGHTS

Family law courts in all fifty states are concerned with the children of divorce, especially when making the decision for custody. The Wisconsin Supreme Court devised a bill of rights guideline for children, used in making custody decision. While this particular bill is not law in Illinois, these basic rights are upheld in Illinois and all fifty states through each state's own laws.

A child has the right to:

○ a continuing relationship with both parents;

○ be treated not as a piece of property, but as a human being recognized to have unique feelings, ideas, and desires consistent with that of an individual;

○ continuing care and proper guidance from each parent;

○ not to be unduly influenced by either parent to view the other parent differently;

○ express love, friendship, and respect for both parents, and freedom from having to hide those stated emotions or made to be ashamed of such;

○ an explanation that the impending action of divorce was in no way caused by the child's actions;

○ continuing, honest feedback with respect to the divorce process and its impact on the changing relationships of the family;

○ maintain regular contact with both parents and a clear explanation for any change in plans or cancellations; and,

○ enjoy a pleasurable relationship with both parents, and never to be employed as a manipulative bargaining tool.

PATERNITY

Many divorce cases involve issues of paternity. It can be as part of an accusation of adultery or in the context of attempting to obtain child support.

All issues of paternity are decided using the *Illinois Parentage Act of 1984*. (750 ILCS 45/1 et seq.) This law creates certain presumptions about the father. The primary presumption is that the man who is married to the natural mother of the child, at the time the child is born or conceived, is the child's father. This presumption is valid even if the marriage is or could be declared invalid.

In order to rebut this presumption, a person must present clear and convincing evidence that someone else fathered the child. In paternity cases, the clear and convincing evidence is the result of a DNA test, which includes an analysis of that test by a DNA expert.

Any divorce case that includes issues of paternity will be considered complex and beyond a person filing without an attorney. For those issues you will need legal assistance.

Child Custody

Who gets custody of the children in a divorce is the most argued over and litigated point in most divorces. Many family law experts have written articles about why this is such a point of contention. Some point to the fact that the person with custody is also entitled to financial support. Others believe that it is because of the emotional upheaval that a parent feels due to the divorce. The divorcing parent sees his or her entire world being turned upside down. This may include moving to a new home, living at a lower financial standard, and losing the dream of a perfect family.

It is understandable that because of such confusing emotions the parent who previously did not have any time for the kids, never changed a diaper, and so on, now wants to prove that he or she is super-parent and hold on to the children. There are also those divorcing parents who are so enraged against their former spouse that they will fight for custody as a way to get even with that spouse, no matter how it hurts the children.

Custody fights can sometimes be defused if you understand the spouse's motivation. The potential super-parent may be appeased with additional visitation or visitation for annual vacation time. The spouse who is only interested in the money may require a larger financial settlement.

For the parent who is willing to use his or her children as pawns to get even with the former spouse, there are no simple solutions. Sometimes these situations respond to professional counseling. For others, time will reduce the rage, and others never stop trying to get revenge on their former spouse, no matter what the cost is.

CUSTODY AGREEMENTS

As part of the divorce settlement agreement, parents should negotiate an agreement for all matters that concern the children, which would include custody, visitation, and support. Most courts will require that the parents or the parents' attorneys do this negotiation outside of the courtroom. It is in the best interest of the children that the parents cooperate on the issue of their children and mutually agree to how the children are raised and where they will live. Of course, any agreement that affects the children will be scrutinized by the court for its adherence to the best interest of the children doctrine.

Because this is an area within the divorce that can take up the most time, it is also a place where you can save the most in legal fees. Parents who work out an agreement without their attorneys can save the time lawyers spend on the same negotiation. Remember that after the divorce, both parents will be required to work together in the raising of their children without having the buffer of an attorney.

See the next chapter for a discussion on Joint Parenting Agreements, which is the legal term for custody and visitation agreements.

FACTORS INFLUENCING CUSTODY

Courts are required by law to look at what would be in the best interest of the child when considering who should get custody of the children in a divorce. As any parent knows, there are many issues that must be considered when making any decisions about children.

The law states that the court shall consider the following factors in determining custody:

- ❂ the wishes of the child's parents;

- ❂ the wishes of the child;

- ❂ where the child has lived;

- ❂ the interaction and interrelationship of the child with parents, siblings, and others of significance;

- ❂ the child's adjustment to his or her home, school, and community;

- ❂ mental and physical health of all involved;

- ❂ physical violence or threat of physical violence by the potential custodian toward the child and others;

- ❂ occurrence of ongoing domestic violence; and,

- ❂ the willingness and ability of each parent to facilitate and encourage a close and continuing relationship between the minor child and the other parent.

These are the same factors the court uses in determining any best interest decision concerning the child. Courts also look at other factors such as a parent's ability to care for the child and keep him or her out of harm's way. Parents who have criminal records due to drug usage or violence are scrutinized in order to determine if the parent has left behind his or her past lawless ways. In addition, a parent's means to provide a safe and stable home for the child is also looked at. This is not to say that the parent who has the most money will automatically get custody of the children. However, a parent who has no means of support and no place to live will probably need to prove to the court that he or she can meet the needs of the children.

EXPECTED CUSTODY CHANGES

Custody laws in Illinois are rumored to be changing in an attempt to eliminate the terms of "custody," "sole custody," "joint custody," and "visitation." Allegedly, the new term will become "parenting time." Laws are gradually adding the word "parenting" to create such terms as "sole parenting" and "joint parenting," but the word "custody" is still the official term.

Other changes will happen, including better court guidelines in determining what is best for the children. These new guidelines will specifically allow the courts to look at the both the willingness and the ability of each parent to place the needs of the child ahead of the parent's own needs. The guidelines will also allow the court to realistically assess the amount of parenting time each person can give and how the responsibilities for the children should be shared.

Another rumored change is the ability for the court to look beyond just the biological parents to set up parenting time accordingly. This would include stepparents, same-sex partners who are not the biological parents, and those people who act in the capacity as parents. Again, these sweeping revisions of custody laws have not yet happened.

CUSTODY LAWS

Illinois laws that cover the custody of children in a divorce include the referenced best interest of child, as well as "Parental Powers—Joint Custody Criteria." (750 ILCS 5/602.1.) Some others include:

- ✪ *Uniform Child Custody Jurisdiction and Enforcement Act* (750 ILCS 36/101);

- ✪ *Illinois Parentage Act* (750 ILCS 40/1 et seq.); and,

- ✪ *Illinois Parentage Act of 1984* (750 ILCS 45/1 et seq.).

Once a court has approved the custody agreement, it cannot be modified for two years unless there is a change in the physical, mental, or emotional health of the custodial parent, or if the children are in danger. Courts require that there be expert testimony to any of these changes before modifying the custody arrangement.

Technically, the custodian determines the children's upbringing, education, health care, and religious training. (750 ILCS 5/608(a).) However, the courts look beyond that meager definition to which parent can provide the most stable, loving environment that will nurture the children. In other words, they go with what is in the best interest of the child.

TYPES OF CUSTODY

The decision of who gets legal custody of the children is a decision made by the court after listening to both parents and the children, and making a custody evaluation. In most states, the court will consider the children's wishes according to his or her age. The older the children, the more weight the court gives their wishes. In situations involving more than one child, Illinois courts tend to keep all siblings together in one household. Remember that each family is unique, and family law courts take the unique needs and wants of each family into consideration in their decisions.

Temporary Custody

Temporary custody is just what it sounds like. The court awards someone to be the legal custodian of the children on a short-term basis. In severe instances, this can arise when there are charges of abuse and the court wants to protect the children. It is typically used after the divorce has been filed with the court, before a final decision has been made. The person who has physical custody of the children technically has temporary custody until the court rules on the custody issue. The court awards temporary custody under the same guidelines it uses in determining physical custody. (750 ILCS 5/603.)

Physical Custody

Physical custody means where the children are to reside. Courts award two types of physical custody—*sole physical custody* and *joint physical custody*.

Sole physical custody. *Sole physical custody* is the most commonly awarded kind of physical custody. The court selects one parent to provide a home for the children. Courts commonly look at where the children have been living, their connection to schools, the community, and their standard of living up to the divorce. In most cases, along with the award of sole physical custody, the court also awards the marital home to that parent. This is to keep the upheaval on the children as limited as possible. Parents should take this into consideration when drafting a custody agreement. They may agree for the custodial parent to keep the marital home until the children reach the age of majority or are no longer in school. At that point, the marital home can be appraised and each parent can receive half the value either by sale to a third party or to one of the parents.

Joint physical custody. Courts can also award *joint physical custody*. In this case, the children reside with each parent for a substantial period of time. The time does not have to be in six month increments, but is for longer than a few weeks. Parents who live at opposite ends of the earth sometime use this to split the school year from annual vacation. However, with more schools going into a staggered schedule, this may not continue to be possible. Parents who live close to each other (within the same school district) seem to be the most successful with this.

It is rare that Illinois courts award this type of physical custody. They find that it is not in the best interest of the children. Parents who agree to joint physical custody should be prepared to present the court with a schedule of when the child will live at each home, the reasons why this is in the best interest of the children, child care professionals who agree, and two very cooperative parents. This is not an easy situation for either parent or children, and can cause the children to resist ever putting down roots.

Legal Custody

Legal custody is the right that the court awards the parent to determine the children's upbringing, education, health care, and religious training. The two types of legal custody are *sole* and *joint*.

Sole Legal Custody. In *sole legal custody*, one parent makes all the decisions concerning the children without any input from the other parent. That other parent is stripped of his or her rights as a parent. Courts will award sole legal custody to one parent in cases when there has been abandonment, abuse, incest, or when the court determines other problems.

Sole legal custody is a serious decision and courts will attempt to resolve problems before making this judgment. Courts more commonly award joint legal custody to both parents with primary residential custody to one parent.

Joint legal custody. *Joint legal custody* involves both parents in the decision-making for the children, and is the arrangement that most Illinois courts favor. Neither parent has superior rights, so both parents are forced to work with each other in raising the children. Most courts believe that having two parents involved in a child's upbringing is in the best interest of the child. However, there are some divorcing parents who will not put aside their animosity for each other to work in cooperation for the children. It is those instances in which the family law court steps in and is forced to make the tough decisions that one or both parents will not like.

The family law court is guided by Illinois law in deciding any custody. For a joint legal custody decision, the court will specifically consider the following:

- the ability of the parents to cooperate effectively and consistently;

- the residential circumstances of each parent; and,

- any other relevant factors.

Parents are required to prepare a Joint Parenting Agreement, which can be part of the Marital Settlement Agreement. This agreement details the rights and responsibilities of each parent in the care of the children's education, health care, and religious training decisions. This Joint Parenting Agreement should also include a provision for mediation if the parents cannot agree, for the physical residence of the children, and the visitation schedule for the children.

INDISCRETIONS OF THE CUSTODIAL PARENT

A parent's conduct is one of the relevant factors that the court looks at when determining custody. While most courts do not want to get involved in making a determination of what is approved sexual conduct, the courts are bound by law to look at the conduct of the custodial parent that has the potential to affect the best interest of the child. In the past, parental sexual misconduct would probably cause the court to deny that parent custody.

In one of the major cases, *In re Marriage of Jarret*, the father won custody of the child, citing the mother's open sexual misconduct. This was affirmed by the Supreme Court of Illinois, which said that the problem was in the moral values that the mother was demonstrating to the children. The mother lived with a man she was not married to, she refused to change this living arrangement, and she discussed this personal relationship with her children. (78 Ill.2d 337, 400 N.E.2d 421, 36 Ill.Dec. 1 (1979).)

More recently, in the case of *In re Marriage of Stone*, the judge stated that sexual misconduct that does not directly affect the child should not be considered, unless there is a possibility that this misconduct will affect the child's environment. (164 Ill. App.3d 1046, 518 N.E.2d 402, 115 Ill. Dec. 877 (1st Dist. 1987).)

In general, courts seem to agree that:

❂ sexual misconduct that happens in front of the child or is discussed with the child will adversely affect the child;

❂ past misconduct without probable future misconduct will not be considered;

❂ sexual misconduct that interferes with the person's ability to perform as a parent will be considered; and,

❂ if it can be proved that the sexual misconduct has no affect on the child, it should not be considered.

What that means to parents who are going for custody is that each court will assess each case on an individual basis, and that parents should be especially careful about their conduct and its affect on their children.

FATHERS AND CHILD CUSTODY

Family law courts are required to select the custodial parent that is in the best interest of the child irregardless of sex. For many years it was assumed that the female parent would be awarded the physical and legal custody of the children. Because of an increase in men who are rightfully demanding that they be awarded custody, mothers are no longer favored. Courts now are giving weight to the parent who served as the children's primary caretaker.

A father who wants to obtain custody of his children should involve himself in all aspects of the children's lives. Courts look at the parent who does such things as take the child to the doctor, change diapers, take off work to care for sick children, discipline, dress the children, and all other instances of parental interaction with their children.

Fathers may be questioned more extensively than mothers by some family courts regarding the father's motivation in wanting custody, his ability to care for younger children, his plans for the future of his children, and his qualifications as a parent. If a father is serious about custody, he should *not* be offended by such inquiries, for there are many people who still cannot understand why a man would want custody. The father should reply in a factual manner, without being indignant or offended, about his relationship with his children. A father who can calmly articulate his love for his children, his plan for the children's future, and his ability to work with the other spouse to raise the children has a much better chance of being awarded custody. Remember, the court is sincerely looking at what is in the best interest of the child.

Fathers interested in custody may be well served by attorneys who concentrate their practice in fathers' rights. These attorneys can be found by bar association referrals, in the phone book, or on the Internet.

An example of a court awarding custody to a father is in a 5th District case decided May 23, 2001. The custody award was modified, changing custody of the child from the mother to the father. The court found that the mother repeatedly interfered with the father's visitation, subjected the child to multiple moves by having five marriages (sometimes to violent men), and that the mother had filed a false charge of sexual molestation. The court stated that the father could provide a "more stable environment" and that the modification of the custody award was in the best interest of the child. (*In re Marriage of Knoche & Meyer*, 322 Ill.App.3d 297, 750 N.E.2d 297, 255 Ill.Dec. 716 (5th Dist. 2001).)

In April 2002, a court transferred custody of the child from the mother, who was awarded legal custody, to the father, who only had visitation rights. The court found that there was evidence that showed that the mother was trying to severely reduce or terminate the time that the father was allowed to visit the child. The court stated that the mother had exercised complete control over the time that the father was allowed to see the child, and had failed to facilitate or encourage a close relationship between the father and the child. (*In re Marriage of Ricketts*, Ill. App. LEXIS 321 (2d Dist. 2002).)

CUSTODY EVALUATIONS

Illinois courts are given several powers to determine custody. These powers are court-ordered interviews, evaluations, investigations, and custody hearings. (750 ILCS 5/604–606.) If the parents have come to an agreement regarding custody and present it to the court, many courts will not proceed with these evaluations. However, some family law courts routinely order custody evaluations (done by professional counselors) or interviews (done by court personnel) in each case that involves a child. It is not an indication that either parent has a problem. It is an indication that more courts are doing a thorough job protecting the children in a divorce.

Ordered Interview

An *ordered interview* in a custody decision can be with the children and the judge or court professional personnel (usually someone with a child psychology background). These professional interviews are becoming the norm with some courts. It does not matter that the parents have cooperated and decided about custody—many courts want an impartial third party to interview the children.

Evaluations   Custody *evaluations* are usually done by a professional counselor or therapist who has spoken to the children, parents, siblings, and other members of the family. The evaluator looks at the behavior and emotional stability of family relationships. There is supposed to be a difference between an evaluator who merely observes the family and a counselor who will also assist the family in problems with the divorce. However, in actual practice, these two roles tend to cross. This is an instance when an attorney who is knowledgeable about the particular workings of a court can assist the parent in preparing for such an evaluation.

Investigations   *Investigations* by third parties into the custodial relationship may be done by a child welfare agency or a professional investigator. It can include information from medical, psychiatric, or other experts who have knowledge about the children. Courts will usually use this method when there has been an application to modify the existing custody arrangement due to a problem with the custodial parent.

Hearing   Finally, a court may hold a *custody hearing*. In this hearing, testimony is taken from concerned people and experts regarding which parent will be awarded custody. A custody hearing will always be held when there is an application to modify an existing custody arrangement. Your attorney can best prepare you for this hearing.

CHILD ABDUCTION

In the past, it was not unusual for a parent who lost a custody fight to take the children across state lines. Now there is a federal law that requires that each state honor the custody orders of other states. The child abductor risks not only state, but federal charges when caught. There is a criminal statute that provides for criminal penalties for child abduction by anyone, unlawful visitation interference, harboring a runaway, and assisting in a child abduction. (720 ILCS 5/10-5.)

There are many groups that can assist a parent in finding abducted children, from those who put children's pictures on milk cartons to groups authorized by the state. Your local police department and child welfare agency can put you in touch with groups that are able to help find abducted children and prosecute their abductors.

Illinois family law courts have made great strides in protecting the children of a divorce, but unfortunately, these abductions still occur. Parents who have legitimate custody problems must pursue the numerous legal avenues available without resorting to removing the child from the state. This action is never an option for the noncustodial parent, both legally and for the best interest of the child.

COUNSELING, MEDIATION, AND PARENTING CLASSES

Most courts have special programs for those divorcing couples who have children. These programs have been instituted under the theory of the best interests of the child as a way to protect the innocent children from the emotional turmoil of a divorce.

Minimally, the majority of courts now require that both parents meet with a counselor who is acting in the capacity of an evaluator of the custody situation. If the couple enters into their own Joint Parenting Agreement (see next chapter for discussion of this), many judges will look more favorably at such an agreement if there is a provision for professional counseling of the children. In contentious divorces, with or without children, it is not unusual for a judge to order that the couple enter into professional counseling for a period of time before the judge will grant a divorce.

Some courts will also order the couple to mediation in order to work out a Joint Parenting Agreement. The rationale behind this is that people who work out an agreement together, not just following the order of the court, are more likely to follow the agreement that they have put their time into.

One of the most successful means of providing professional assistance to parents who are divorcing are the parenting classes that many counties are making mandatory for those with minor children. These professionally run classes help the parents deal with the effects that divorce has upon the minor children. As with most counseling, the parents will probably be charged a fee to attend these sessions. However, parents must realize that for the emotional well-being of them and their children, these classes are well worth the fee.

Child Visitation

Visitation is the scheduled time that the noncustodial parent has with his or her children. Ideally, both parents should decide the *visitation schedule* for their children and present it to the court in their Joint Parenting Agreement, which is part of their Marital Settlement Agreement. (see Appendix E.)

THE COURT'S VIEW

Courts will award the noncustodial parent visitation rights unless the court determines that these visits are detrimental to the best interests of the children. This means that denying a natural parent visitation rights is only done when there is evidence that these visits will endanger the children's physical, emotional, or mental health.

In the past, some parents have used denial of visitation as a way to get back at their spouse. Many have even falsely accused the spouse of criminal acts with the children in order to deny that spouse any visitation. Courts today take a very dim view of that tactic. It is a criminal offense for a parent to prevent the other parent from court-ordered visits. (720 ILCS 5/10-5.5.) Family law courts say that it is important that children have the right to a relationship with both parents, and that both parents have input into the raising of their child.

THE CHILD'S WISHES

Depending on age, most courts will take into consideration children's wishes as to visitation with the noncustodial parent. The older, more mature the child, the more his or her wishes are considered by the court. However, the court will always balance this with what is in the best interest of the child.

Many times children in a divorce will be upset by the questioning of attorneys as to how they feel about the noncustodial parent, which is why some judges will take the children into their *chambers* (private office) to do the questioning (called *in camera*). It is also not unusual for one parent to exert undue influence over the children, causing additional feelings of guilt and confusion in an effort to get even with their former spouse. Most courts take this into consideration when making a visitation decision.

JOINT PARENTING AGREEMENTS

The court will issue a Joint Parenting Order, which will include both custody and visitation schedules. In order to save money and have more control over your life, it may be beneficial for you and your spouse to enter into a Joint Parenting Agreement that you will submit to the court. These agreements will be scrutinized by the courts under the best interest of the child theory, and the court may change what you have agreed upon. However, parents who take the time to negotiate a Parenting Agreement before going to court will be in a better position to have their decisions heard and acted upon.

A Joint Parenting Agreement will minimally have sections setting forth both the type of custody and the terms of a visitation schedule. Many agreements also include items such as:

- ✪ how to change the agreement;

- ✪ how to resolve disputes;

- ✪ when one parent can take the children out of Illinois;

- ✪ the education of the children;

- ✪ the children's time with other important relatives of both parents;

- ✪ parent's involvement in school or sports activities;

- ✪ the children's religious education;

- ✪ special needs of the children; and,

- ✪ any other item that a parent feels is important.

VISITATION FACTORS

Most parents are overwhelmed when they are required to sit down and draw up a schedule of when they will see their children. It can be a double blow. On top of losing your spouse, you now are limited as to the time you are allowed to see your children. There is nothing that can be said to eliminate this feeling. Know that it is a terrible hurt, but that it is necessary in order to get on with the divorce.

Above all, *do not* refuse to participate in building a visitation schedule with your soon-to-be ex-spouse. If you leave it to the court to decide when you can visit, you will be disappointed. The law does not require a certain amount of visitation time for the noncustodial parent, and that means the judge has no guide but the testimony of both parents and children in setting a visitation schedule. As with many other aspects of a divorce, if your spouse is not cooperating or you are having problems going through the divorce process, seek legal assistance.

THINGS TO CONSIDER
WHEN DRAFTING A VISITATION SCHEDULE

✪ Your work schedule

✪ Your other family or community obligations

✪ The children's school schedule

✪ Days that you hold special (holidays, birthdays)

✪ Vacations

✪ Days off

✪ Children's educational needs (time for homework, tutoring)

✪ Medical needs

✪ Children's other activities (sports, clubs)

✪ What the children want

✪ Changes in future needs

✪ Time for yourself

VISITATION SCHEDULES

One of the most important things that a parent can do when seeking a divorce is to work out a fair and reasonable visitation schedule with the other parent. Some courts have found that *fair and reasonable* means:

✪ visitation does not interfere with the child's schooling or after school activities;

✪ both parents get important holidays on an equal basis; and,

✪ the schedule does not unreasonably favor one parent over the other.

It is essential that both parents cooperate to determine what visitation schedule will work for them. Schedules should contain who transports the children for the visits, times of drop off and pick up, and other details. There should be provisions (usually a swap in dates) for times when the children are too sick to go for a visit, times when the parent is ill and cannot take the child, and other emergencies that will come up in daily life.

Another item of this schedule is which parent gets visitation on which holidays. If both parents celebrate the holiday on the same day, perhaps a schedule in which each parent gets the child for that holiday on an every other year basis is needed. Not just legal holidays, but birthdays of both parents and children should be considered.

There are some events that are usually overlooked when drawing up a visitation schedule. There are the emergencies, such as a grandparent's funeral that the noncustodial parent would like the children to attend. Or happier occasions, such as a parent receiving an award, graduating, or other event where it would mean a great deal to both the child and the parent for the child to attend. There are also non-planned events in the child's life, such as recitals, plays, and awards, where it is important for both parents to be in attendance. While parents cannot plan for every event, the schedule should allow for changes and promote cooperation.

NOTE: *The more detailed a visitation schedule is, the better.*

CHANGING SCHEDULES

Visitation schedules can be *modified* (changed) at any time by the court. This usually requires a drastic change in conduct or circumstances that can be shown by clear evidence to the court. Visitation schedules can be permanently changed or temporarily changed depending on a particular date or a certain occurrence. Any issue that was brought to the court's attention in the divorce procedure or in other visitation modifications cannot be used.

Example:
A parent's prior felony conviction that was in evidence when the divorce court initially considered visitation cannot be the basis for changing the visitation schedule, there must be a recent change.

The most common circumstances in which the courts have modified visitation schedules are:

- ✪ repeatedly not following the visitation schedule;

- ✪ repeated failures to return the child to the custodial parent on time;

- ✪ teaching the child immoral or illegal acts; or,

- ✪ the noncustodial parent being convicted of a crime.

In the instances where the noncustodial parent has been accused of child abuse courts tend to *suspend* (postpone) visitation until the charges of abuse have been decided.

COMMON MISCONCEPTIONS

You have probably heard people say that because the noncustodial parent has not paid support the custodial parent is going to prevent visitation. The custodial parent should not interfere with visitation, unless under the advice of his or her attorney, without a court order that allows this. Interfering in court-ordered visitation can be a criminal offense.

If the child refuses to go on visitations with the other parent, it is up to both parents to find the reasons behind this. There are many reasons why a child throws a tantrum about visitation, which include:

- ✪ the noncustodial parent may be stricter;

- ✪ the child wants to stay in his or her home; or,

- ✪ the child wants to show loyalty to the custodial parent.

It can even be as simple as whose home has better toys. Before the custodial parent seeks to have the visitation schedule changed, the child may need to speak to a professional in child psychology. If the reason that the child does not want to be with the noncustodial parent is because of abuse, the custodial parent needs to speak with the authorities.

As stated, a custodial parent who attempts to destroy the relationship between the child and the noncustodial parent may be considered guilty of interference or alienation of the parental relationship. When this interference or alienation is severe, courts can transfer custody. The term *Parental Alienation Syndrome* is used to describe the situation in which one parent engages in an active scheme to deny any type of relationship between the other parent and the child.

Just as the above activity can cause legal problems with the custodial parent, a noncustodial parent who decides to stop paying child support when denied visitation can also be in trouble with the courts. The noncustodial parent who wants to stop paying child support should first contact an attorney for assistance. Not paying court-ordered child support payments can be considered a criminal offense.

Child Support

Parents may be ordered to pay child support regardless of their fault or misconduct during the breakup of the marriage. Like all other elements in a divorce, this does not have to be left up to the court to decide. Child support can be decided by mutual agreement of the parents. However, Illinois law provides guidelines as to the amount of support each child should get. Absent unique circumstances, that guideline is the minimum amount that will be awarded.

Some courts will allow amounts *lower* than these guidelines in situations when both parties have agreed to the lower amount and there are provable unique circumstances that the amount is warranted. Also, courts may award *more* than the guideline amounts when the court determines that this is in the best interest of the children.

HOW CHILD SUPPORT IS CALCULATED

The law requires a certain minimum amount of child support that is to be paid by the noncustodial parent to the custodial parent. This amount is calculated as a percentage of the noncustodial parent's net earnings.

NOTE: *For a quick estimate on child support, go to* ***www.divorcehq. com/calculators/il_supportcalc.shtml.***

The law that governs child support is complex and lengthy. (750 ILCS 5/505.) However, the general breakdown for calculating support is as follows.

Number of Children	Percent of Supporting Party's Net Income
1	20%
2	28%
3	32%
4	40%
5	45%
6 or more	50%

Varying From the Guidelines

The basic guidelines will be applied in each case, unless it is determined that using these guidelines would be inappropriate or not in the best interests of the child when considering the following:

✪ the financial resources and needs of the child;

✪ the financial resources and needs of the custodial parent;

✪ the standard of living the child would have enjoyed had the marriage not been dissolved;

✪ the physical and emotional condition of the child and his or her educational needs; and,

✪ the financial resources and needs of the noncustodial parent.

Net Income

Net income is defined as the total of all income from all sources, minus the following deductions:

✪ federal income tax;

✪ state income tax;

✪ Social Security (FICA payments);

✪   mandatory retirement contributions required by law or as a condition of employment;

✪   union dues;

✪   dependent and individual health and hospitalization insurance premiums;

✪   prior obligations of support or maintenance actually paid pursuant to a court order; and,

✪   expenditures for repayment of debts that represent reasonable and necessary expenses.

FACTORS CONSIDERED FOR INITIAL SUPPORT ORDER

Courts take into consideration many factors when determining if the child support should be higher, lower, or consistent with the percentage guidelines. This is another area where the courts are directed by the *best interests of the child* law.

The following are some of the factors that the courts take into consideration:

✪   the lifestyle the child would have if the parents remained married;

✪   the financial resources of both parents and the child, including income and earning capabilities;

✪   tax liabilities, employment stability, and employment potential of the parents;

✪   the possibility of the child getting employment;

✪   the child's educational need and ability to obtain scholarships or grants;

✪   the cooperation between the parents on visitation and custody;

✪   the impact on the parents to maintain two households; and,

✪   the age and health of the parents and the child.

MEDICAL INSURANCE FOR THE CHILDREN

Medical insurance is usually addressed as part of the Marital Settlement Agreement. Courts are increasingly looking at this issue as a must-have for the children, even during the divorce process. In deciding who pays for this, courts look at who can provide the medical coverage from an employer, who has provided past medical coverage, who can provide the most comprehensive coverage, and the costs.

It is not uncommon nowadays for one parent to be ordered to pay half of the total premiums that the other parent is paying for health coverage for the children. Remember that medical coverage includes health, eye, dental, hospitalization, and life insurance.

MODIFICATION OF CHILD SUPPORT

Courts generally do not consider modifying child support. One reason it is difficult to alter this support is because family law courts take such pains in making sure that the support award is fair and in the best interests of the children to begin with.

Unless specifically agreed to in a Marital Settlement Agreement, child support can only be modified when:

✪   the original agreement was miscalculated;

✪   there is a need for child health care; or,

✪   there is a *substantial change in circumstances*.

NOTE: *Courts will allow child support modifications to be done at any-time in an emergency, to protect the best interests of the child.*

Factors Considered for Modification

In making a modification to an existing child support order, the courts consider many items. In addition to those just listed, the most recent cases have considered:

- the income of the new spouses for both parents;

- the additional assets that are available for support;

- the increase in the cost of living and costs of raising a child; and,

- the new family responsibilities of both spouses.

In the past, the additional income generated by the new spouse of the custodial parent would have no effect on the amount paid in child support. Some recent cases indicate that this will not always be the case.

In one case, *Street v. Street*, 325 Ill.App.3d 108, 756 N.E.2d 887 (2001), the court stated that there is a trend to move away from the traditional views that do not consider the parent's current spouse's income when deciding a motion to increase child support. In this case, the income of the wife's current husband was taken into consideration when the wife attempted to get her ex-husband to pay more child support for the child's college education. The court would not increase the amount that the ex-husband was to pay in child support due to the income of the current husband, which was also supporting the child.

Substantial Change in Circumstances

Changes in circumstances allow for a spouse with a decreased ability to pay because of job termination, downsizing, and so on, to apply to the court for a modification. Courts are not in favor of lowering the amount of child support and will do a very detailed review on requests to lower the amount. Some courts will lower or suspend the amount of child support only on a temporary basis, with the full amount to be paid at a later time.

Courts generally do not favor voluntary career changes that lessen the parent's ability to pay the full amount of child support. In the case *In re Marriage of Dall*, 212 Ill.App.3d 95, 569 N.E.2d 1131, 155 Ill. Dec. 520 (5th Dist. 1991), the court would not modify the amount of child support because the father resigned from his job without other prospects of employment in an attempt to reduce the amount he paid for support. However, the courts did allow a temporary reduction in the amount a father paid for child support when he quit a dead-end job for another job that started out at a lower pay, but had the potential for greater income. (*In re Marriage of Webber*, 191 Ill.App.3d 327, 547 N.E.2d 749, 138 Ill. Dec. 582 (4th Dist. 1989).)

Courts will also not allow child support (or spousal support) to be discharged due to *bankruptcy*. Courts have temporarily suspended support payments with the full amount to be repaid (sometimes with interest) at a future date. If the court determines that the bankruptcy was filed in order to avoid support payments, courts will not discharge the payments, and they sometimes file charges against the spouse who has attempted to avoid support.

When the noncustodial parent receives a substantial increase in income, custodial parents often file cases to increase the amount of child support. In making a decision on this type of case, most courts will look at the same factors stated earlier, plus the economic lifestyle of the noncustodial parent. If that parent has remarried and now has children by a new spouse, the courts may decline to increase the amount of child support. This is judged on a case-by-case basis, and the custodial parent cannot be sure that his or her request for increased child support will be allowed by the court.

> **NOTE:** *Courts demand that all modification requests be made in **good faith**. Currently, more courts are filing charges against parents who they believe are attempting to fraudulently avoid paying child support.*

COLLEGE EXPENSES

The law states that child support ends when the child reaches the age of *emancipation*, which is 18 years old in Illinois. However, support can be required for a child who continues his or her education into college. It is best that the Marital Settlement Agreement contain a clause that provides for support of the child and a sharing of college expenses, even if the parents are sure that the child will not go on to college. Included in this clause should be a provision that the child will apply for scholarships, grants, and other financial awards to pay part of tuition. Parents may also want to address such items as:

- ✪ a requirement that the child get part-time or summer jobs to pay part of tuition;

- ✪ the amount of input that the parent paying support can make in the selection of the school; and,

- ✪ where the child will live during the school year.

NOTE: *When deciding on the amount of college support, remember to include books, supplies, dues, transportation, telephone, and other expenses.*

If college expenses were not part of the original Marital Settlement Agreement at the time of divorce, then the custodial parent will be required to return to the court and request a modification. At this point, the court will review the factors in consideration of modification and decide if additional support should be awarded.

SUPPORT FOR NON-MINOR CHILDREN

It is a sad fact of life that some children will need financial support for the rest of their lives. These are children who are mentally or physically disabled and cannot support themselves. This type of support is usually ordered by the court through the Marital Settlement Agreement at the time of divorce or in a request for modification at a later date. Although the court still reviews all the considerations that are listed earlier, courts will not leave such children to fend for themselves without some financial support.

ENFORCEMENT OF CHILD SUPPORT

A parent cannot get even with a former spouse by not paying child support. Besides being terribly unfair to the children, not paying legally ordered child support is against the law and may force the delinquent parent into a variety of penalties not just from state law, but also from federal laws.

Federal Child Support Laws

Under the *Federal Child Support Act*, all states (including Illinois) have enacted laws to effectively enforce child support orders. (United States Code Annotated (U.S.C.A.), Title 42, Sec. 666.) This federal law authorizes federal institutions to enforce state orders for withholding funds from a parent who has been found delinquent in payment of child support orders. The *Full Faith and Credit for Child Support Orders* requires every state to enforce child support orders from other states. (U.S.C.A., Title 28, Sec. 1738B.)

The Child Support Recovery Act of 1992 (U.S.C.A., Title 18, Sec. 228) enables punishment for the spouse who:

✪ willfully fails to pay child support for a child (who lives in another state) for a period of more than one year or in an amount of more than $5,000;

✪ goes to another state or country in an attempt to evade the payment of back child support that has been due for more than one year or is in the amount of more than $5,000; or,

✪ willfully fails to pay child support for a child in another state for a period of more than two years or in the amount of more than $10,000.

This punishment ranges from a fine and six months imprisonment for a first offense, to a fine and imprisonment for up to two years.

These laws give the spouse who is owed child support the ability to collect from the spouse who has fled to another state. They make the issue of unpaid child support a serious crime and have helped many in collecting back child support.

While these federal laws do help, one major problem for the spouse who is owed money is that the interstate enforcement of these laws usually requires the assistance of at least one attorney and sometimes several. Getting out-of-state courts to enforce support orders usually requires a hearing where an attorney who is licensed in that state will present the case to the court. Currently, there are some interstate organizations who are beginning to address this issue and hopefully will soon be able to offer low-cost assistance.

Illinois Child Support Enforcement

The state of Illinois takes the issue of child support very seriously. Like the federal laws, not paying child support can result in fines, interest on back due support payments, imprisonment, and other actions.

For those who are chronically behind in child support payment, the custodial spouse may ask the court to order that the payments be made to the court. This will give the court a record of payments and delinquencies, and eliminate the need for contact between two antagonistic ex-spouses. Do not wait to ask the court to do this. If the noncustodial spouse has exhibited this behavior on those temporary support payments prior to the divorce decree being final, then amend your complaint to have support payments paid to the court.

Illinois courts will also allow child support to be taken as an *automatic wage deduction* from the paying parent's pay check. Back child support can be obtained by *garnishing* wages, garnishing tax refunds, and attaching other assets. A noncustodial parent who has not paid child support for more than ninety days may also have his or her driver's license suspended until the back child support is paid.

Your first step in obtaining past due child support should be to formally request assistance from the State of Illinois. You can do this by following the instructions on the Illinois Department of Child Support Enforcement at **www.ilchildsupport.com** or calling them at 800-447-4278. This agency is for both parents who receive public assistance and for those who do not receive this assistance. The website provides a tremendous amount of information for anyone who is having problems collecting child support, including regional locations that are in the area where you live.

Another great source for information on enforcing child support orders is at **www.divorcehq.com/deadbeat.html**.

Grandparents' Rights After Divorce

The rights of grandparents are in two areas—visitation and custody. Almost every state will allow grandparents certain visitation rights. Visitation is done on the basis of biological connection, so only those who are the biological grandparents will qualify. In this area, as in everything that affects children, the court will be guided by what is in the best interests of the children.

Currently, this area of law is volatile, as new cases are defining and changing the court's interpretation of the existing laws and new laws are being written. This is because the grandparents today are younger, more involved with their grandchildren, and are willing or financially able to go into court to fight for continued involvement with their grandchildren. The country is also experiencing an increased number of grandparents who have taken responsibility for raising their grandchildren due to various circumstances. Courts are now promoting the rights of grandparents as a way to encourage the extended family and in the best interests of the children.

A divorce decree, which includes a visitation schedule for both parents, can—and should—also include a visitation schedule for the grandparents and other members of the extended family. If the husband and wife include this visitation schedule within the divorce decree, the grandparents will not be put into the tough position of having to request a court order such visitation.

THE LAW AFFECTING GRANDPARENT VISITATION

Since this book was originally written, there have been many changes to the law that affect grandparent visitation. This law has been reduced, built up, changed, and then reduced again. If you are a grandparent who is not able to have visitation with your grandchildren due to a divorce of the parents, you will probably need to get the assistance of an experienced family law attorney who concentrates on this type of law. The law is complex and ever changing. The changes will only continue as society's ideas on what makes up a family unit change.

The current law dealing with grandparent visitation primarily resides at 750 ILCS 5/607 (a-5) (1) through (5). This section of the law is only a part of the very complex statute that addresses visitation on minor children in a divorce.

In August 2004, Illinois Governor Blagojevich signed House Bill 4318, which reestablished a grandparent's ability to legally petition for court imposed visitation under the current law. This bill was put into effect on January 1, 2005. However, the courts are constantly reinterpreting the law that affects the rights of grandparents to petition for visitation. Be sure to check for any changes in the law regarding grandparents' rights.

The new aspects of the *Grandparent Visitation Act* (2005) include the following.

❂   Grandparents must show unreasonable denial of visitation by the parent of the child. This means that the grandparents must first make attempts at a reasonable visitation, and the parent must decline the reasonable visitation. When looking at what is a *reasonable visitation*, the court would probably reject such things as visiting a child at an hour when the child is normally sleeping, having the child sent to another state instead of the grandparents coming to the child, or any other visitation that could negatively affect the child. Courts are also looking at alternate means of visitation, such as phone calls and communication via the Internet. A recent case stated that overnight visits are not reasonable.

○ In order for grandparents to get court-ordered visitation, one parent must agree to that visitation. If both parents object to the grandparents' visitation, the court will not force the parents to change their minds. The courts believe that this would be an infringement on the rights of parents to raise their children both in marriage and in divorce.

○ Children who are subject to the Juvenile Court system are exempt from this act. In these cases, the Juvenile Court will make the decision as to who is allowed visitation and custody. If the Juvenile Court determined that both parents are unable to care for the children, the Juvenile Court may award custody to the grandparents.

○ Grandparents no longer just have to prove that their visits are in the best interests of the child—they also have to prove that the parent's action denying them visitation is harmful to the child's mental, physical, or emotional health. This is more of a hair-splitting legal issue. Under the prior version of the law, all a grandparent needed to say was that the child would benefit from visitation by the grandparent. In actual cases, most judges asked the additional questions about why the parent wanted to deny grandparent visitation and how that hurt the children.

○ The law has given the judges additional factors to consider when determining whether to grant grandparent visitation. These are:

• preference of the child;

• physical and mental health of the child;

• physical and mental health of the grandparents;

- length and quality of the prior relationship with the grand-parents;

- good faith of both parents and grandparents;

- quantity of the visits requested;

- potential adverse effect from the visits;

- if the child lived with the grandparents for six months or had frequent visits over the past twelve months; and,

- any evidence that the loss of the relationship between the child and grandparent would cause the child harm.

VISITATION

Illinois law specifically allows the court to grant reasonable visita-tions of a grandparent, depending upon the best interest of the child. (750 ILCS 5/607(b).) Although the law is directed at allowing grandparent visitation, many courts have limited this visitation. Courts have a *presumption* in favor of the natural parents. This means that if the natural parents are against grandparent visita-tion, that grandparent must be prepared to fight in court and prove that his or her continued connection to the grandchild is in the best interest of the child.

Courts take several items into consideration in determining if grand-parent visitation is in the best interest of the child, such as:

- the relationship between the child and the grandparents;

- the relationship between each of the child's natural parents and the grandparents;

- the total time the grandparents have spent with the child;

- the time since the child had contact with the grandparents;

- ✪ the effect of the grandparents visitation on the relationship between the child and his or her natural parents;

- ✪ the custody arrangement between the natural parents;

- ✪ the good faith of the grandparents in seeking visitation;

- ✪ the physical and mental health of the grandparents;

- ✪ any history of physical, emotional, or sexual abuse or neglect by the grandparents; and,

- ✪ any other factor which would effect the best interests of the child.

This is an exhausting list and the courts back this with investigations, interviews, and hearings. Courts will favor the natural parents in many cases. They will back away from awarding grandparent visitation if that visitation is strongly opposed by one or both of the natural parents, and it appears that the visitation would harm the relationship between the child and the natural parent.

Obtaining Court-Ordered Visitation

If a grandparent cannot privately obtain visitation to a grandchild after a divorce, then the grandparent can petition the court for such visitation. In court ordered visitation, the court sets a specific schedule of time that the grandchildren spend with the grandparents. The court will assume that in this situation there is a certain amount of animosity between the natural parents and grandparents, or else this would have been settled without court intervention.

Grandparents should be encouraged to file for visitations when a divorce and custody fight has become especially bitter, in order to give the children some stability. In this type of bitter divorce, it is not unusual for the custodial parent to deny anyone in the noncustodial family visitation of the children.

Testimony. Grandparents who want the court to set up a visitation schedule should be prepared to prove that contact with them would be in the best interest of the children. Attorneys can prove this with testimony of expert witnesses, who are usually professional psychiatrists or psychologists. Courts usually will appoint their own mental health professionals to interview the grandparents and the children involved. These professionals will testify that it is in the best interests of the children to keep in contact with their grandparents and that such contact can provide emotional support for the children.

There will also be testimony as to the current relationship between the grandparents and grandchildren. The ultimate deciding factor will be if the visitation is in the best interest of the children. Grandparents who go into court to request visitation must be able to prove this.

NOTE: *Grandparents who wish to have visitation with grandchildren after a divorce should take the time to attempt negotiations with the custodial parent first. Grandparents may even request that a professional mediator attempt visitation negotiations. Only after all avenues of negotiation are exhausted should you going into court to force visitation.*

Negotiating Visitation

Before filing court documents, it is wise for the grandparents to approach the custodial parent in an attempt to work out some level of contact with the child. Custodial parents may be hesitant to set up visitation schedules with the grandparents because they live many miles or states away, due to the young age of the grandchildren, or because of other logical reasons. Email, letters, and phone calls between the grandparents and grandchildren can be an alternate connection until face to face visitation can be arranged. This type of alternate connection can be the first step for the custodial parent in trusting that the intention of the grandparents is also for the best interest of the children.

CUSTODY

Grandparent custody is becoming more frequent. In one case, the court awarded the grandparents custody using what was in the best interest of the children as a guide. In this case, the child had lived with his grandparents most of his life. The mother was granted custody of the child in 1990 and she immediately moved in with her parents. In 1996, the mother left for another state and the grandparents were legally appointed as guardians of the child. In 1997, the father petitioned the court to obtain custody of the child. After custody evaluations of the grandparents by court-appointed and private mental health professionals, and a three-day court hearing, the court found that the grandparents provided the best place for the child. (*In re Marriage of Dafoe*, 324 Ill.App.3d 254, 754 N.E.2d 419.)

This case came after several courts had sought to limit the visitation of grandparents. It is a good example of the number of obstacles that a grandparent must overcome to go against the presumption for the natural parent. In this case, the grandparents had:

- been appointed guardians by one of the natural parents;

- housed the child for several years;

- provided support for the child's medical condition; and,

- gone through many mental health evaluations to prove that they were supportive of their grandchild.

In another case, the child's maternal grandmother was awarded custody. Here, the father of the child was convicted of murdering the child's mother and was sent to jail. He appointed his parents as guardian of the child so that he could keep in contact with the child. After a long court fight that was appealed, the court awarded the maternal grandmother custody under the best interest of the child theory. (*In re A.W.J. (Tawrel v. Patterson, et al.)*, 316 Ill.App.3d 91, 736 N.E.2d 716.)

These cases show that courts are inclined to award custody of the children only in special cases. Courts are guided by the best interest of the child theory in these cases. Several courts have been accused of more strictly applying this standard in cases when grandparents want custody than when the noncustodial parent files for custody. Grandparents who wish to pursue custody should be aware of this and plan for a long, tough fight.

GRANDPARENTS RAISING GRANDCHILDREN

It is not unusual for the grandparent to be called upon to raise the grandchildren, especially when the parents have divorced. Sometimes this custody will happen because the parent who previously had custody is no longer able to care for the children for any number of reasons. To those grandparents raising their grandchildren, the following provides information on obtaining financial assistance in Illinois.

- ✪ There are temporary grants provided to children under the *Temporary Assistance to Needy Families* program. While the grant may be small, it can be a monthly stipend that includes medical assistance and, if the grandparent works outside the home, may even include day care assistance. This is not for families who are receiving foster care benefits or child support. The grandparent must prove that the child is living with him or her and that there is a blood relationship. Some of these benefits can last until the child turns age 18. This program is administered by the Illinois Department of Human Services. Call 800-843-6154 or go online at **www.dhs.state.il.us**.

- ✪ A grandchild may also be eligible for benefits on the work record of a parent, or the grandchild may be able to obtain some benefits as a child of retired grandparents. This program is administered by the Social Security Administration. Call 800-772-1212 or go online at **www.socialsecurity.gov**.

- ✪ A low-income grandparent with a grandchild under 5 years old may be eligible for assistance from the *Women, Infants, and Children* program or even the food stamps program. This program is administered by the Illinois Department of Human Services. Call 800-843-6154 or go online at **www.dhs.state.il.us**.

- ✪ The court may order one of the parents to pay child support to the grandparents to support the grandchild. If the court has ordered child support, the grandparents can turn to the Illinois Child Support Enforcement Department. Call 800-447-4278 or go online at **www.ilchildsupport.com/ customer_service_cs.html**.

✪ Grandparents can also obtain medical insurance for grandchildren under the Illinois KidCare program. This program is administered by the Illinois Department of Human Services. Call 800-843-6154 or go online at **www.dhs.state.il.us**. You can also contact:

KidCare
P.O. Box 19122
Springfield, IL 62794-9122
866-468-7543
www.kidcareillinois.com

✪ Illinois also has many local support groups for grandparents raising grandchildren. These groups can help you find the best resources for your needs. Contact Illinois Department of Aging, Grandparents Raising Grandchildren, at **www.state.il.us/aging/1directory/grg_support.pdf**.

Other sources of grandparent support include the following.

✪ The Illinois Family Caregiver Support Program
www.state.il.us/aging/2aaa/aaa-main.htm

✪ AARP Grandparent Information Center
601 E Street, NW
Washington, DC 20049
888-687-2277
www.aarp.org/life/grandparents/helpraising

✪ U.S. Government Administration on Aging
800-333-4636
www.firstgov.gov/topics/grandparents.shtml

The Military Divorce

A military divorce occurs when one of the parties is an active service member. This is not a legal term, but indicates that this type of divorce is different. Those entering a military divorce not only need to comply with state law, but with the federal laws that cover military pay and pensions.

Just like civilian couples, military couples must comply with the law of the state where they are filing for divorce. The state selected to file for divorce depends on who files, as in civilian divorces. Many states are relaxing their residency requirements for those in the military who are stationed in their states. Due to differences in how state courts handle military divorces, especially in terms of awarding military retired pay, a service person may wish to position him- or herself in a particular state if possible. Military couples not only must go through the procedural process required by state law, but they also must endure duty assignments that may prolong the time it takes to finalize a divorce.

SELECTING AN ATTORNEY

The most critical thing that a military person must do to obtain a divorce is hire an attorney who is experienced in handling a military divorce. Your military pay is affected by your divorce, and your divorce decree is required to incorporate accurate federal law. Do not just assume that your local JAG office will provide you with all the information that you need to process your own divorce. This is a very specialized area that absolutely requires prior experience. You will need to assess an attorney's experience in this area prior to hiring him or her.

One attorney who is familiar with military divorces has suggested that the military person ask the attorney questions that only a person who is familiar with military procedure would know, to determine the level of experience. Two examples of such a questions are "What does TDY mean?" and "Does this state require an SBP?"

In addition to the items listed in Chapter 4 in this book, you will need to provide additional information at your initial consultation. This includes information such as pay grade, status, years of service, special pays and allowances, and any other military information that may affect your pay and retirement.

All branches of service offer some legal assistance to enlisted personnel and their families when it is feasible. You may wish to consult with your service to see what is actually available to you. Additionally, some local bar associations are making certain legal assistance available for those in the military.

USFSPA

The law that applies to divorces of military personnel is the *Uniformed Services Former Spouse's Protection Act* (USFSPA). Other statutes that can affect a military divorce are the *Service Member Civil Relief Act* (SCRA) and the procedures found at 10 U.S.C. §§ 1062 and 1072.

NOTE: *Make no mistake, just because you read the laws mentioned here does not mean that you can handle your own military* *divorce. This is not a legal action that should be done by any person who does not have experience in military divorces. This divorce not only affects you immediately, but also will affect your finances when you retire from the service.*

The entire Uniformed Services Former Spouse's Protection Act is reproduced in Appendix B. (20 U.S.C. §1408.) You may wish to review this before meeting with an attorney. Your attorney can assist you in understanding this law. The USFSPA applies to all active duty, reserve, guard, and retired military, including the U.S. Coast Guard, U.S. Public Health Service (USPHS), and the National Oceanographic and Atmospheric Administration (NOAA).

The USFSPA gives the right to distribute military retired pay to a former spouse and provides a method of enforcing these orders through the Department of Defense. The former spouse does not have an automatic right to a portion of the military retired pay. It must be awarded as property in the *final decree* (court order) of divorce, dissolution, annulment, or legal separation. The USFSPA also provides a method of enforcing current child support and alimony that has been awarded by the state in the same final decree.

The retired pay award must express the payment in a dollar amount or as a percentage of disposable retired pay. *Disposable retired pay* is gross retired pay minus allowable deductions. The award can be up to 50% of the retirement pay. The awards of retirement pay, child support, and alimony should not exceed a total of 65% of disposal retirement pay; however, a few state courts have ignored that limit. Putting the award of retired pay in the appropriate court order means a *Qualified Domestic Relations Order* is not required as it is with non-military pension awards.

The service member's rights under the *Soldiers' and Sailors' Relief Act of 1940* (SSCRA) must be observed by the state court. This act does require certain orders for dividing retired pay as property. It also requires that the service member and spouse be married to each other for a minimum of ten years, during which time the service person performed a minimum of ten years creditable military service (this is commonly called the 10/10 rule).

NOTE: *Those who have twenty years of marriage during which time the service member had twenty years of creditable military service receive many benefits and financial allowances during the marriage. These generous benefits end for the non-service member upon divorce. This financial loss should be considered and be part of the divorce negotiations of the non-service person.*

The USFSPA 1408(h) provides benefits to the former spouse who is a victim of abuse by the service member. As a result of the spousal or child abuse, that service member loses the right to retired pay.

Common Mistakes about the USFSPA

There are several cases that point out common mistakes made in a military divorce regarding this law. The most confusing aspect is the computation of retirement pay that the former spouse will get. The USFSPA does not require a particular formula. Calculating the amount depends on the type of service, how much time was spent on active duty, if it was an early retirement, and the rank at the time of retirement (not at the date of the divorce, which is the date used in state law). The *Defense Finance and Accounting Service* (DFAS) will supply the number of years of creditable service.

The USFSPA does not allow the former spouse to get disability pay, which is to be deducted from the amount before the calculation of the share sent to the former spouse. However, due to the confusion caused by the lack of a particular formula in the statute and the slowness of the VA in responding to disability pay disputes, some former spouses do, in fact, get a portion of the disability pay.

Another problem occurs when the former spouse remarries. According to the USFSPA, the award of military retirement pay ends upon the remarriage of the former spouse. However, it appears that all states are not complying with this law. Because the USFSPA allows the former spouse to reapply for the award of military retirement pay if his or her remarriage ends, combined with the slow movement in obtaining documents on military retirement pay, this continues to be an area of contention in some cases.

The USFSPA was intended to provide for a long-term spouse who supported the military member's career. It has become a point of confusion due to the variety of different interpretations by state courts.

This is the primary reason why you need an experienced attorney to represent you in a military divorce.

Applying for Payments under USFSPA

Both the USFSPA and SSCRA require specific information be included in the *final decree* (court order) of divorce, dissolution, annulment, or legal separation. Generally, the spouses must prove that they have met the 10/10 rule requirements. This can be done by submitting a court copy of the marriage certificate and military documents that show the beginning service date. If there is an award for child support, the court order must contain the birth dates of all children and court copies of the children's birth certificates should be included.

The former spouse should also complete the application (DD Form 2293) and include a copy of the final decree that is certified by the clerk of the court where the decree was obtained. This should be served within ninety days of the date of the final decree to:

Defense Finance and Accounting Service
Cleveland Center
Code L
P.O. Box 998002
Cleveland, Ohio 44199-8002

The DFAS processes your application, makes sure that your final decree complies with the federal laws, and provides the service member with the appropriate notification. The service member has thirty days from the date of that notice to file evidence that will prevent such payments. The USFSPA requires that payments must begin no later than ninety days after ordered in the final decree. Payments are made once a month in coordination with the monthly retired pay cycle.

SURVIVOR BENEFIT PLAN COVERAGE

The biggest misconception about the *Survivor Benefit Plan* (SBP) is that former spouses who were beneficiaries during marriage will continue to be beneficiaries after the divorce. This is not true. The SBP should be addressed in the divorce negotiations and must be included in the final decree.

The service member may elect what is called *former spouse coverage* in the SBP. This is restricted to those former spouses who were originally covered as a spouse beneficiary and is available to divorced service persons who become eligible for retired pay.

The former spouse can also initiate his or her own SBP coverage, which is referred to as *deemed election*. This deemed election must be included in the final decree. The Defense Finance and Accounting Service must be notified of this deemed election within one year of the final decree. The current customer service number for the Defense Finance and Accounting Service is 800-321-1080.

Other Financial Matters to be Considered

If you are seriously considering divorce, you should prepare yourself for dealing with the family financial matters without the assistance of your spouse. It would be best if you and your spouse had shared decisions and information on finances throughout your marriage, but in many marriages this is not the case. Before filing for a divorce, while you still have access to the family's financial records, you should make copies of certain records. Income tax returns for the last five years will give the most complete picture of the financial status of the marriage.

You should also have information on insurance policies that you and your spouse have. This includes health, auto, home, and life insurance. At minimum, you should have the name of the insurance carrier, what the policy covers, and which spouse's name is on the policy. You may also want to acquire other information regarding investments, pensions, property, and other assets that are owned by either spouse.

INSURANCE

Once you get a divorce, there are several insurance issues that you need to deal with. The first thing you need to do is to notify the insurance companies where you have policies of your divorce. You probably will want to change the beneficiary from your spouse to your children or to another member of your family. Some insurance companies will require a copy of your divorce decree.

You may be ordered by the court to purchase additional life insurance on yourself if you are paying child support and list the children as beneficiaries on this policy. This is to guarantee that the children will continue to be taken care of financially after you are gone. If you are the custodial parent, you may wish to get additional life insurance that names the children as beneficiaries for the same financial protection.

Disability Income Insurance

After a divorce, you will probably be the sole breadwinner of the family. You may wish to invest in some type of disability income insurance that will pay monthly income to you should you become unable to work due to being disabled. Most of these types of insurance policies will only pay a portion of your salary if you become disabled; the average is about 65% of your salary.

Some employers offer this type of insurance with the employees paying all of the premiums. Policies offered by employers are usually at lower group rates and sometimes will allow you to purchase a policy that would cover close to 100% of your salary if you become disabled. A policy offered by your employer may also offer you the broadest type of coverage; that is, the insurance policy's definition of what is a disability may include more than what is usually considered a disability. It may include things like short-term disability for those times when the disability that prevents you from working is expected to end within a certain time. Examples of short-term disability include being in the hospital for a period of time, rehabilitation from an injury or illness, or being confined to bed for a period of time. These are situations in which the person will recover.

Social Security disability payments are usually inadequate for most people and usually do not cover any disability that is short-term. Qualifying for Social Security benefits can be difficult and may require several hearings and appeals with the Social Security office just to get benefits started. Typically, Social Security disability benefits cover fatal illnesses and those physical or mental disabilities that are serious enough that you cannot work for at least twelve months. Social Security benefits usually do not begin until after the first six months of your illness.

Medical Insurance

If you have children, you probably have already negotiated who will carry the medical insurance for the children. It is very important that this insurance is kept in effect by whichever parent is ordered to provide medical insurance. If your spouse pays for this insurance and you are the custodial parent, make sure that you obtain the proper insurance information for your children. This information may be a written document or in the form of a card that authorizes medical coverage. Usually, the employer-provided medical insurance plans have specific enrollment periods once a year, and issue new authorization documents or cards for each year.

If your spouse had you on his or her employer-provided medical insurance, you will probably need to find your own insurance unless providing your health insurance was part of the marital settlement. The majority of policies will no longer cover an ex-spouse once the divorce or legal separation is final. Employer-provided insurance is usually best because employers get a group policy with a group rate, even if the employee must pay all the premiums. If your employer does not provide insurance, or if you are self-employed or unemployed, you will have to obtain individual medial insurance. Do not skimp on this expense, especially if you are the custodial parent—maintaining your health is very important.

You may qualify for *COBRA*—continued coverage in an employer's group health plan that the federal law requires for those who lose their jobs or are ineligible to participate in the plan due to divorce. COBRA applies to both the ex-spouse and the children of an employee. In this type of insurance, the employer does not pay any of the premiums for the insurance, but the insurance can be bought at the low group rate. Not all companies provide for COBRA, so you will need to check with the employer.

Auto and Home Insurance

You must notify all insurance companies, such as auto and home, upon your legal separation or divorce. If you do not notify them it may adversely affect your policy and you may lose some coverage. After a divorce you may find that your auto insurance is more expensive. You may lose those multi-car discounts or other incentives. On the other hand, your auto insurance may be lower if your spouse had numerous accidents or tickets.

Remember, Illinois requires that your carry auto insurance. If you get into an accident or are stopped by the police and cannot prove that you have auto insurance, you will probably be required to appear in court, be fined, and be made to buy insurance quickly. Besides the costs of being caught without insurance, having an accident without insurance can cost you everything you own if you are at fault. It is not worth the risk to drive without insurance.

If you are awarded the marital home, you will also be responsible for home insurance, or if you are renting, renter's insurance. If you want to reduce the cost of this insurance, your insurance company can probably give you some ideas. Usually having a smoke detector, a fire extinguisher, deadbolt locks, or other security devices will help to lower premiums. If you have a mortgage, your mortgage company will require that you carry an insurance policy on your home. If you rent, your landlord probably will not have any insurance on the contents of your unit. As with auto insurance, is makes good sense to keep your home insured. A fire can destroy your home and all your belongings, and without insurance they will not be replaced.

TAXES

Taxes play a very significant role in getting a divorce. You and your spouse may even agree to postpone your divorce into the next year due to the effect that divorce has on income tax.

The last day you are married in a calendar year will determine if you can file a joint return or must file as single for the entire year. There is usually no gain or loss when one spouse transfers real property to the other spouse, which can save capital gains tax. Spousal support or maintenance is deductible for the payor and included as income to the payee. Child support payments are not deductible for the payor, but are still included as income for the custodial parent. The custodial parent has the right to claim the children as exemptions to offset this, but in many cases the noncustodial parent wants this to make up for not being able to claim child support as a deduction.

Other tax concerns of people going through a divorce are items such as one spouse's liability for mistakes and underreporting that was done exclusively by the other spouse. In that case, you may be able to claim relief from the tax liability under the *Innocent Spouse* rules that the IRS uses. Because these rules are subject to frequent changes, you should contact a tax professional or go to **www.irs.gov** to view what is required to be considered an Innocent Spouse.

Another frequent concern is taxes on maintenance (alimony). These amounts are currently deductible by the payor and are included as income by the person getting the money *only* if there is a legal order of the court requiring the payment of maintenance. Private maintenance agreements are not subject to this tax method.

Taxes are a very complex subject. In cases of divorce when children are involved, they become even more complex. This is definitely an area where you need to consult with a tax expert. If you can, do consult a tax expert before you file for a divorce.

ESTATE PLANNING

Remember that you are legally married until your divorce becomes final. If your spouse dies without a will after you have filed for a divorce but before it becomes final, you are the legal spouse with control over the estate. This can happen even if one spouse has a will that leaves everything to someone other than the spouse. Typically, spouses are designated as executors, trustees, and beneficiaries on wills, trusts, life insurance, retirement accounts, and other financial documents that pay out upon death.

If one spouse is disabled or severely injured before the divorce becomes final, it is usually the other spouse who will have control over all the finances. In many cases, as part of an estate plan, a spouse will sign a *health care power of attorney* that designates the other spouse as the person who has the right to make his or her health care decisions. These decisions can range from what type of care to give to real life and death questions.

The question becomes one of timing and how to protect yourself during the period between filing for a divorce and it becoming final. If you have an estate planning attorney who drafted the original documents, you may wish to have new documents drawn up or you may ask your divorce attorney for assistance. If you do not have a will, now may be a good time to get one naming someone other than your spouse. It may also be a good time to change the beneficiary designation on bank accounts, investment accounts, real property, and any other assets.

PENSIONS

Under Illinois law, pensions earned during a marriage are considered to be joint property. The court will not automatically give you this benefit—you must ask for it. In order to do so, you will need to know several pieces of information. You will need to know where your spouse was employed, what pension plan or retirement plan he or she participated in, and where to contact the pension administrator. This can be a monumental task and is usually best left to your lawyer. Unfortunately, without a lawyer's letter regarding a pending divorce, most pension administrators will not provide a spouse with information.

Once your lawyer obtains the above information, he or she will need to draft a *Qualified Domestic Relations Order* (QDRO), which asserts your rights to part of your spouse's pension, provides the appropriate mathematical calculations of your portion, and gives proper legal notification to the pension plan or retirement administrator. All of this must be done in accordance with the pension plan or retirement plan's own rules. The court that grants your divorce will review this document and make it a judicial order of the court. That means that the court will enforce this order.

A QDRO is a complex document that is written individually for each divorce. You cannot use a QDRO of a friend or a neighbor. There are no legal forms for a QDRO, as it must be individualized to the particular pension or retirement plan and the parties involved.

For more information on pensions and divorce contact the Women's Institute for a Secure Retirement at **www.wiserwoman.org**, and the American Association of Retired Persons at **www.aarp.org**.

SOCIAL SECURITY

Another important financial issue for a divorced spouse will be Social Security. This can effect the newly divorced in various ways. A divorced spouse may be entitled to Social Security benefits under the *Surviving Divorced Wife/Husband* program or under the *Divorced Mother/Father* program. In these cases, there must be a valid marriage and the worker must have died fully insured by Social Security. Other requirements include that the marriage lasted a minimum of ten years and that the remaining spouse is either sixty years old, is disabled, or has a child of the deceased spouse in his or her care.

For either divorced spouse benefits or child benefits, the first step is to file an application with the local Social Security Office. For more information contact Social Security at 800-772-1212 or online at **www.socialsecurity.gov**.

Final Thoughts

This book was written with a goal to broadly cover the very complex area of divorce law in Illinois. Since the law changes daily, what we have presented may have changed by the time you read this. Before you embark on any legal procedure, especially a divorce, do your research. Contact the county clerk where you intend to file and ask questions. Ask questions of those in the courthouse, libraries, and of lawyers who offer free consultations.

If you are still undecided about going through a divorce, get some professional assistance from counselors. There is free assistance out there, but you will have to search for it. Look at all your options and your alternatives. Take your time and make decisions based on knowledge and logical reasoning.

Going through a divorce is hard. It takes courage to make changes in your life even when you know these changes must be done. Society and the media tend to glorify being part of a married couple as the primary goal for everyone. The reality is that a single person can be as fulfilled, happy, and satisfied as a married person. There is nothing more pitiful, sad, or wasteful than two people who are chained to an unhappy marriage. Life is too short to be unhappy.

Glossary

A

abandonment. When one spouse leaves the marital home without consent for a period of one year.

absent parent. The noncustodial parent who pays child support but is physically absent from the residence where the child lives.

abuse. Under the law, it includes physical abuse, harassment, intimidation, interfering with a person's liberty, or willful deprivation.

adversarial divorce. A divorce in which one spouse asserts that the other spouse is responsible for the breakup of the marriage. The opposite of a no-fault divorce.

affidavit. A statement of facts in writing that is made under oath. It is usually witnessed and signed by a notary.

affirmative obligation. A requirement that is put into a law. In a divorce, a person who receives maintenance or alimony for a period of time in order to become financially independent must obtain the training or skills to become self-sufficient.

alimony. Financial support paid to one spouse by another spouse. It can be temporary or permanent. Also called maintenance or spousal support.

alternative dispute resolutions. Ways to resolve differences; usually refers to arbitration and mediation.

annulment. A legal action causing the marriage to be treated as if it never took place.

answer. A legal document used to respond to a legal complaint or legal petition.

antenuptial agreement. Also call a prenuptial agreement, a written agreement signed by two people before they marry that limits rights to property, support, and other matters in case of a divorce.

appeal. A legal procedure to get a higher court to review a ruling.

appearance. A legal document that lets the court know who is representing a party to court suit.

arbitration. Letting a professional arbitrator work with the parties to resolve the dispute. The arbitrator is usually not a judge, but the decision can be binding on the parties.

automatic wage deduction. A court-ordered method to obtain child support. The support is taken directly from the noncustodial parent's paycheck by the employer.

B

bench warrant. An order by a judge for a person's arrest. Commonly used in cases where the person did not obey a previous court order, such as an order of protection.

best interest of the child. A legal directive that requires the courts to look at what is in the best interest of the child when determining the type of custody and which parent is selected to have legal custody of children in a divorce.

bigamy. Being married to several people at the same time. Can occur when a person marries another before his or her divorce has become final by judgment of a court. This is an illegal act.

C

charging lien. A lien brought by an attorney to get his or her fees by preventing the sale of an asset until the fees are paid.

Children's Bill of Rights. List of rights granted to children written by the Wisconsin Supreme Court. It is not law in Illinois but is used as guidelines by many family law courts.

child support. Money given by one parent to another in order to support the children.

circuit. Refers to the judicial system in Illinois, which is divided into twenty-two geographical regions.

citation. A legal summons or the numbering system used to identify a law.

common law marriage. Marriage without a license, which is not recognized in Illinois.

community property. The law in some states (not Illinois) by which each spouse owns 50% of all the marital property.

community property states. The states of Arizona, California, Idaho, Louisiana, Nevada, New Mexico, Texas, and Washington.

complaint. Legal document filed with the court that states why the case was filed and what the party wants.

contempt of court. A violation of a request or order of a court. It can be a criminal offense that results in jail time or a monetary fine.

contested. Divorces where the parties are disputing certain legal issues.

counterclaim. A response to a Petition for Divorce that can state different grounds or request other relief, such as support or property arrangements.

court docket. The calendar or schedule of cases in a particular court.

cross-examination. Asking questions of a witness or a party to a lawsuit who was called to stand by the other side.

custody. When referring to children, it is who makes decisions for the minor children as to education, religion, health care, and daily living.

D

deadbeat. The term used by the State of Illinois to describe parents who do not pay their child support obligations.

declaration. Testimony that is written and given under oath.

decree. The final decision made by the court, as in divorce decree.

default. Failure to do something on time. In a divorce, it usually refers to a failure to file a legal document by a certain date.

default order or judgment. An order or judgment made on only the plaintiff's or petitioner's complaint because there was no response from the other person (defendant or respondent) within a certain time.

defendant. Also known as respondent, the spouse who has the lawsuit brought against him or her by the other spouse.

deferred compensation package. All retirement assets (such as pension, 401(k), or IRA).

deposition. Testimony given under oath outside a courtroom.

direct examination. The examination of a witness or party by the side who called that person to the stand.

discovery. A court-ordered period, done before the actual trial, when attorneys for both sides obtain information about the case.

dissolution of marriage. The legal judgment that ends a marriage.

docket. *See court docket.*

domestic relations court. *See family court.*

domestic violence. Illegal conduct, emotional or physical, against another member of a family.

domicile. The place where a person lives and is considered as primary residence by the IRS.

E

emancipation. When a child is legally not considered a minor.

equitable division. The name of the court system used by the majority of states to divide the marital property in a divorce.

estate. The interest in property or the actual property of a deceased person.

evidence. Physical proof, affidavits, and testimony presented to a court in support of a particular legal issue.

exhibits. Term for physical things presented as evidence.

ex parte. Communication between the court and only one side of a lawsuit.

exploitation. Taking another person's assets by an illegal method, such as fraud.

F

family court. The court that hears divorce and other family-related suits. Sometimes called the domestic relations court.

fees. What a lawyer charges his or her client for legal services.

felony. A serious criminal offense where the sentence can include jail time.

file. To place a legal document in the official custody of a representative of the court. General term usually used to indicate that the case has been started.

financial declaration. *See income and expense declaration.*

foreign order. Any court order that was issued by a state other than Illinois or in another country.

G

garnishment. A method to enforce a support order by taking the money directly from the supporter's paycheck. *See automatic wage deduction.*

good faith. A theory used in all areas of law. Acts done in good faith are those things done with out evil intent and without knowledge that the act is in violation of the law. An example would be the innocent person who marries someone who already has a spouse. This innocent person acted in good faith even though the marriage resulted in bigamy.

grounds. The legal basis for a divorce.

guardian ad litem. A person appointed by a judge to legally assess and represent a person who is legally unable to speak for themselves either due to age or illness. In a divorce, a judge may appoint a guardian ad litem to represent the children.

H

harassment. Unwelcome actions or words that are meant to inflict stress or fear on another.

hearing. A proceeding that takes place in a courtroom in front of a judge.

hearsay. What someone claims he or she was told by some other person. Usually cannot be used as a statement of fact in court.

I

in camera. Legal proceeding held in a judge's chambers with or without the participating parties. Frequently done when children testify.

income and expense declaration. This lists a person's income, assets, expenses, and liabilities. Usually used to determine child support, spousal support, or the division of property. (Required by most courts.) Also called a financial declaration.

indigent. Term used by the federal government that means that a person makes less money than what is considered by the government as a living wage. This amount changes annually. As a rule of thumb, if a person qualifies for government assistance and is not required to pay income tax, they are probably considered indigent by the federal government.

injunction. A court order that prevents someone from doing some act.

interference with personal liberty. Forcing a person to do something they do not want to do or preventing them from doing something they want to do. More serious than parental discipline.

interrogatories. Questions in writing from the other side in a case. These questions require written answers that are sworn under oath.

intimidation of a dependent. A type of abuse in which the innocent dependent is forced to do something for fear of physical abuse.

irreconcilable differences. Grounds for divorce in Illinois. Also referred to as the no-fault divorce.

J

joint legal custody. When both parents make the decisions for minor children as to education, religion, health care, and daily living.

joint parenting agreement. A document that both parties create that deals with visitation, custody, and all other issues regarding minor children in a divorce.

joint physical custody. When parents share the physical custody of the children. Children actually have two homes and live in each on a set schedule.

joint property. Property that is held by more than one person.

judgment of divorce. *See decree.*

jurisdiction. The power of the court to rule on a legal issue.

L

legal custody. The right to make decisions for minor children as to education, religion, health care, and daily living.

legal separation. A legal procedure in which the parties get court assistance on a separation. Used primarily due to religious concerns and to get court-ordered support.

lien. A legal claim that is put on a piece of property due to an unpaid debt. In divorces it is common for an attorney to put a lien on the marital home to be paid legal fees past due.

litigation. Process of fighting a legal dispute in the court system.

lump-sum alimony. Spousal support that is paid in one fixed amount or in several installments to reach that amount.

M

maintenance. *See alimony.*

marital debt. Debts acquired by both the husband and wife after marriage and before divorce.

marital property. All the property that legally belongs to both spouses.

marital settlement agreement. A written agreement signed by both spouses that divides property, determines support, specifies custody, and addresses child visitation.

mediation. A non-adversarial procedure to assist those divorcing to reach a settlement or to reconcile.

mediator. An independent professional who presides over a mediation.

mental cruelty. Grounds for divorce in Illinois. You will be required to describe the behavior of your spouse that has caused you to feel depressed, upset, or nervous, and state that you did not provoke this behavior

minor children. Children under the age of 18.

misdemeanor. Less serious crime than a felony. Can still result in jail time.

modification. A court order that changes the terms of an existing order. Usually used to change support or custody orders.

motion. A legal document that is presented to the court asking that the court issue a legal order or instruction. An example in a divorce case is for one side to make a motion to the court to force the other side to produce certain financial documents.

N

neglect. Failure to give sufficient and appropriate care.

no-fault divorce. In Illinois, a divorce that is based on the grounds of irreconcilable differences.

noncustodial parent. The parent that does not have primary custody of the child.

nonmarital debt. Debts acquired by both the husband and wife before the marriage or after the date of the divorce.

nonmarital property. Property that is judged to be that of either the husband or wife solely.

O

objection. A verbal interruption of an attorney at a trial or deposition. Done when the interrupting attorney believes that something inappropriate was said.

order. A court ruling on a disputed issue.

orders of protection. A court order that legally restricts a person from contact with another. Frequently used in domestic violence situations in an effort to keep the two parties apart.

order to show cause. A court order that requires a party to a legal action to appear in court and present evidence as to why the court should not do something.

P

palimony. Support paid to someone who was never a legal spouse.

party. A plaintiff or defendant (petitioner or respondent) in a legal action.

paternity. Legal, biological relationship between father and child.

perjury. Lying under oath.

petition. Another word for complaint. Written request to the court that usually begins a lawsuit.

petitioner. The person who files for the divorce; the person who initiates the paperwork to the court.

physical abuse. Conduct that creates an immediate risk of physical harm to another.

physical cruelty. Ground for divorce in Illinois. You will be required to describe acts of physical violence, your injuries, and show any evidence, such as pictures or medical reports, of these injuries.

plaintiff. Person who files the suit against the defendant.

pleadings. This is another term for the formal written documents that are filed with the court.

postnuptial agreement. An agreement between husband and wife, which is in writing and states their rights in case of a divorce.

praecipe. A word for an order asking the court to act.

prenuptial agreement. *See antenuptial agreement.*

primary caretaker. The person a child lives with most of the time. Depending upon the court this may also refer to the parent who has custody of the child.

privilege. Client's right not to disclose communications between him or her and his or her attorney, doctor, priest, etc.

pro se. Acting as your own attorney.

Q

qualified domestic relations order (QDRO). A court ruling that divides a pension as part of marital assets.

quitclaim. A release to a legal claim usually used by one spouse to give the marital home to the other spouse.

R

reciprocity. Cooperation between states and countries to enforce orders of support and custody.

rehabilitative alimony. Support that helps a spouse become financially self-sufficient.

rehabilitative maintenance. Maintenance or alimony that is given only for a certain length of time. During that time, the person who is receiving the maintenance is required by law to obtain training and skills in order to become financially self-sufficient. Courts do require that the person receiving this type of maintenance obtain the training or skills needed

remedy. What a petitioner wants the judge to order the respondent to do.

residence. The place were a person lives, considered his or her home.

respondent. The person who is served with papers in a divorce.

response. *See answer.*

restraining order. A legal injunction that keeps someone from doing something.

restricted visitation. Order by the court that the time the children spend with the noncustodial parent be either limited in time or frequency, or that the visits include another person whose job it is to watch over the children during the visit. Courts normally use this only when the noncustodial parent poses a serious physical or emotional threat to the children.

Revised Uniform Reciprocal Enforcement of Support Act (RURESA). Allows courts of one state to enforce support orders from another state.

S

sanctions. Court-ordered punishment.

separate property. In a divorce, the property that belongs solely to either husband or wife.

serve a summons. *See service of process.*

service of process (service). Act of giving the other side in a lawsuit a copy of the complaint and summons.

settlement agreement. *See marital settlement agreement.*

sole custody. When one parent is awarded both physical and legal custody.

specialties/specialist. Some states provide for attorneys to become specialists in certain areas of law. The specialties can be in family law, intellectual property, or any number of legal areas available. Illinois does not use this term in the area of family law.

spousal support. *See alimony.*

statute. Another word for a law.

stipulation. An agreement on a legal issue between both parties.

subpoena. Document that is served on a party or witness in a lawsuit.

subpoena duces tecum. Legal command to produce document or other tangible items in court.

supervised visitation. *See restricted visitation.*

summons. A written notification that a legal action has been filed in the court system.

T

temporary custody.   Routinely awarded custody to one parent while waiting for the court to make its final decision. It legally allows that parent to make decisions for the children.

temporary orders.   A court order that lasts only for a short period of time. Commonly used in divorce situations to keep one party from doing something, such as taking the couple's children out of the state. This can also be referred to as a TRO—a Temporary Restraining Order—because is restrains a certain action.

testimony.   Statements made under oath at a hearing, deposition, or trial.

transcript.   A written copy of testimony given.

trial.   Final hearing in a courtroom to decide issues in a case.

U

uncontested.   Divorces in which there are no disputes as to the legal issues.

Uniform Reciprocal Enforcement of Support Act (URESA).   A law that enables one state to assist another in establishing or enforcing a child support order.

V

visitation.   The right of the noncustodial parent to see his or her children.

visitation schedule.   List of dates and time of visitation. (Usually found in the Marital Settlement Agreement.)

W

wage assignments or withholding. A court order that requires the employer to deduct child support from a paycheck.

willful deprivation. Denying dependent food, medical care, shelter, or any needed services.

State of Illinois Judicial Circuit Courts

Petitions for Divorce and all other legal matters dealing with the divorce are heard by the Circuit Courts. Each Circuit Court has its own procedure and forms that a person is required to use in a divorce case.

To use this Appendix, look up your county and find out which Judicial Circuit your county belongs to. Then, get the information about your Judicial Circuit from the second part of this Appendix. Use the addresses, phone numbers, and websites (where available) to get information from your particular Circuit Court.

CIRCUIT COURTS BY COUNTY

County	Judicial Circuit
Adams	Eighth Judicial Circuit
Alexander	First Judicial Circuit
Bond	Third Judicial Circuit
Boone	Seventeenth Judicial Circuit
Brown	Eighth Judicial Circuit

County	Judicial Circuit
Bureau	Thirteenth Judicial Circuit
Calhoun	Eighth Judicial Circuit
Carroll	Fifteenth Judicial Circuit
Cass	Eighth Judicial Circuit
Champaign	Sixth Judicial Circuit
Christian	Fourth Judicial Circuit
Clark	Fifth Judicial Circuit
Clay	Fourth Judicial Circuit
Clinton	Fourth Judicial Circuit
Coles	Fifth Judicial Circuit
Cook	Cook County Circuit
Crawford	Second Judicial Circuit
Cumberland	Fifth Judicial Circuit
DeKalb	Sixteenth Judicial Circuit
DeWitt	Sixth Judicial Circuit
Douglas	Sixth Judicial Circuit
DuPage	Eighteenth Judicial Circuit
Edgar	Fifth Judicial Circuit
Edwards	Second Judicial Circuit
Effingham	Fourth Judicial Circuit
Fayette	Fourth Judicial Circuit
Ford	Eleventh Judicial Circuit
Franklin	Second Judicial Circuit
Fulton	Ninth Judicial Circuit
Gallatin	Second Judicial Circuit
Greene	Seventh Judicial Circuit
Grundy	Thirteenth Judicial Circuit
Hamilton	Second Judicial Circuit

County	Judicial Circuit
Hancock	Ninth Judicial Circuit
Hardin	Second Judicial Circuit
Henderson	Ninth Judicial Circuit
Henry	Fourteenth Judicial Circuit
Iroquois	Twenty-first Judicial Circuit
Jackson	First Judicial Circuit
Jasper	Fourth Judicial Circuit
Jefferson	Second Judicial Circuit
Jersey	Seventh Judicial Circuit
Jo Daviess	Fifteenth Judicial Circuit
Johnson	First Judicial Circuit
Kane	Sixteenth Judicial Circuit
Kankakee	Twenty-first Judicial Circuit
Kendall	Sixteenth Judicial Circuit
Knox	Ninth Judicial Circuit
Lake	Nineteenth Judicial Circuit
LaSalle	Thirteenth Judicial Circuit
Lawrence	Second Judicial Circuit
Lee	Fifteenth Judicial Circuit
Livingston	Eleventh Judicial Circuit
Logan	Eleventh Judicial Circuit
McDonough	Ninth Judicial Circuit
McHenry	Nineteenth Judicial Circuit
McLean	Eleventh Judicial Circuit
Macon	Sixth Judicial Circuit
Macoupin	Seventh Judicial Circuit
Madison	Third Judicial Circuit
Marion	Fourth Judicial Circuit

County	Judicial Circuit
Marshall	Tenth Judicial Circuit
Mason	Eighth Judicial Circuit
Massac	First Judicial Circuit
Menard	Eighth Judicial Circuit
Mercer	Fourteenth Judicial Circuit
Monroe	Twentieth Judicial Circuit
Montgomery	Fourth Judicial Circuit
Morgan	Seventh Judicial Circuit
Moultrie	Sixth Judicial Circuit
Ogle	Fifteenth Judicial Circuit
Peoria	Tenth Judicial Circuit
Perry	Twentieth Judicial Circuit
Piatt	Sixth Judicial Circuit
Pike	Eighth Judicial Circuit
Pope	First Judicial Circuit
Pulaski	First Judicial Circuit
Putnam	Tenth Judicial Circuit
Randolph	Twentieth Judicial Circuit
Richland	Second Judicial Circuit
Rock Island	Fourteenth Judicial Circuit
St. Clair	Twentieth Judicial Circuit
Saline	First Judicial Circuit
Sangamon	Seventh Judicial Circuit
Schuyler	Eighth Judicial Circuit
Scott	Seventh Judicial Circuit
Shelby	Fourth Judicial Circuit
Stark	Tenth Judicial Circuit
Stephenson	Fifteenth Judicial Circuit

County	Judicial Circuit
Tazewell	Tenth Judicial Circuit
Union	First Judicial Circuit
Vermilion	Fifth Judicial Circuit
Wabash	Second Judicial Circuit
Warren	Ninth Judicial Circuit
Washington	Twenty-first Judicial Circuit
Wayne	Second Judicial Circuit
White	Second Judicial Circuit
Whiteside	Fourteenth Judicial Circuit
Will	Twelfth Judicial Circuit
Williamson	First Judicial Circuit
Winnebago	Seventeenth Judicial Circuit
Woodford	Eleventh Judicial Circuit

CIRCUIT COURTS BY JUDICIAL DISTRICT

www.state.il.us/court/CircuitCourts

Circuit Court of Cook County

Cook County
Dorothy A. Brown
50 West Washington
Room 1001
Chicago, IL 60602-1305
Phone: 312-603-5030
Fax: 312-603-2041
www.cookcountyclerkofcourt.org

First Judicial Circuit

Alexander County
Sharon McGinness
2000 Washington
Cairo, IL 62914-1717
Phone: 618-734-0107
Fax: 618-734-7003

Jackson County
Cindy R. Svanda
10th and Walnut
P.O. Box 730
Murphysboro, IL 62966-0730
Phone: 618-687-7300
Fax: 618-684-6378
www.co.jackson.il.us
www.circuitclerk.co.jackson.il.us

Johnson County
Neal E. Watkins
Courthouse Square
P.O. Box 517
Vienna, IL 62995-0517
Phone: 618-658-4751
Fax: 618-658-2908

Massac County
Larry Grace
Superman Square
P.O. Box 152
Metropolis, IL 62960-1888
Phone: 618-524-5011
Fax: 618-524-4850

Pope County
Penni R. Taber
Main Street
P.O. Box 438
Golconda, IL 62938-0502
Phone: 618-683-3941
Fax: 618-683-3018

Pulaski County
Cindy Kennedy
500 Illinois Avenue
P.O. Box 88
Mound City, IL 62963-0088
Phone: 618-748-9300
Fax: 618-748-9329

Saline County
Randy Nyberg
10 East Poplar
Harrisburg, IL 62946-1553
Phone: 618-253-5096
Fax: 618-253-3904

Union County
Lorraine Moreland
309 West Market Street
Room 101
Jonesboro, IL 62952
Phone: 618-833-5913
Fax: 618-833-5223

Williamson County
Stuart Hall
200 West Jefferson
Marion, IL 62959-2494
Phone: 618-997-1301
Fax: 618-998-9401

Second Judicial Circuit
www.illinoissecondcircuit.info

Crawford County
Denise Utterback
Court Street
P.O. Box 655
Robinson, IL 62454-0655
Phone: 618-544-3512
Fax: 618-546-5628

Edwards County
Patsy Taylor
50 East Main Street
Albion, IL 62806-1262
Phone: 618-445-2016
Fax: 618-445-4943

Franklin County
Donna Sevenski
On the Square
P.O. Box 485
Benton, IL 62812-2264
Phone: 618-439-2011
Fax: 618-439-4119

Gallatin County
Mona L. Moore
Lincoln Boulevard
P.O. Box 249
Shawneetown, IL 62984-0249
Phone: 618-269-3140
Fax: 618-269-4324

Hamilton County
Bobbi Oxford
100 South Jackson Street
McLeansboro, IL 62859-1490
Phone: 618-643-3224
Fax: 618-643-3455

Hardin County
Diana Hubbard
Main and Market
P.O. Box 308
Elizabethtown, IL 62931-0308
Phone: 618-287-2735
Fax: 618-287-2713

Jefferson County
Gene Bolerjack
10th and Broadway
Box 1266
Mt. Vernon, IL 62864-1266
Phone: 618-244-8007
Fax: 618-244-8029

Lawrence County
Peggy Frederick
1100 State Street
Lawrenceville, IL 62439-2390
Phone: 618-943-2815
Fax: 618-943-5205

Richland County
Sandy Franklin
103 West Main Street
#21
Olney, IL 62450-2170
Phone: 618-392-2151
Fax: 618-392-5041

Wabash County
Angela K. Crum
401 Market
P.O. Drawer 997
Mt. Carmel, IL 62863
Phone: 618-262-5362
Fax: 618-263-4441

Wayne County
Sharon L. Gualdoni
301 East Main Street
P.O. Box 96
Fairfield, IL 62837-0096
Phone: 618-842-7684
Fax: 618-842-2556

White County
Ellen I. Pettijohn
301 East Main Street
P.O. Box 310
Carmi, IL 62821-0310
Phone: 618-382-2321
Fax: 618-382-2322

Third Judicial Circuit

Bond County
John K. King
200 West College
Greenville, IL 62246-1057
Phone: 618-664-3208
Fax: 618-664-2257
www.johnkking.com

Madison County
Matt Melucci
P155 North Main
Edwardsville, IL 62025-1955
Phone: 618-692-6240
Fax: 618-692-0676
www.co.madison.il.us/
circuitclerk/circuitclerk.htm

Fourth Judicial Circuit

Christian County
Donna Castelli
On the Square
Box 617
Taylorville, IL 62568-0617
Phone: 217-824-4966
Fax: 217-824-5030

Clay County
Rita L. Porter
111 Chestnut
P.O. Box 100
Louisville, IL 62858-0100
Phone: 618-665-3523
Fax: 618-665-3543

Clinton County
Jeff Luebbers
850 Fairfax
Carlyle, IL 62231-0407
Phone: 618 594 2415
Fax: 618-594-0197
www.clintonco.org/circuit_
   clerk.htm

Effingham County
Becky Jansen
100 East Jefferson
#101
P.O. Box 586
Effingham, IL 62401-0586
Phone: 217-342-4065
Fax: 217-342-6183
www.co.effingham.il.us/
   circuitclerk.html

Fayette County
Marsha Wodtka
221 South Seventh
Vandalia, IL 62471-2755
Phone: 618-283-5009
Fax: 618-283-4490

Jasper County
Sheryl Frederick
100 West Jourdan
Newton, IL 62448-1973
Phone: 618-783-2524
Fax: 618-783-8626

Marion County
Ronda Yates
100 Main
P.O. Box 130
Salem, IL 62881-0130
Phone: 618-548-3856
Fax: 618-548-2358

Montgomery County
Mary Webb
120 North Main Street
Box C
Hillsboro, IL 62049-0210
Phone: 217-532-9546
Fax: 217-532-9614
www.courts.montgomery.k12.il.
   us/circuitclerk.htm

Shelby County
Cheryl Roley
P.O. Box 469
Shelbyville, IL 62565-0469
Phone: 217-774-4212
Fax: 217-774-4109

Fifth Judicial Circuit

Clark County
Terri Reynolds
501 Archer Avenue
Box 187
Marshall, IL 62441-0187
Phone: 217-826-2811
Fax: 217-826-1391
www.clarkcountyil.org/circuit_
   court.htm

Coles County
Vicki Kirkpatrick
6th and Jackson
Box 48
Charleston, IL 61920-0048
Phone: 217-348-0516
Fax: 217-348-7324

Cumberland County
Golda Dunn
Courthouse Square
Box 145
Toledo, IL 62468-0145
Phone: 217-849-3601
Fax: 217-849-2655

Edgar County
Karen Halloran
115 West Court Street
Paris, IL 61944-1739
Phone: 217-466-7447
Fax: 217-466-7443

Vermilion County
Susan Miller
7 North Vermilion Street
Danville, IL 61832-5806
Phone: 217-554-7730
Fax: 217-554-7728
www.co.vermilion.il.us/
    circlk.htm

Sixth Judicial Circuit

Champaign County
Linda S. Frank
101 East Main Street
Urbana, IL 61801-2736
Phone: 217-384-3725
Fax: 217-384-1261
www.cccircuitclerk.com

DeWitt County
Kathy A. Weiss
201 West Washington Street
Clinton, IL 61727-0439
Phone: 217-935-2195
Fax: 217-935-3310

Douglas County
Julie Mills
401 South Center
P.O. Box 50
Tuscola, IL 61953-0050
Phone: 217-253-2352
Fax: 217-253-9006

Macon County
Kathy Hott
253 East Wood Street
Decatur, IL 62523-1489
Phone: 217-424-1454
Fax: 217-424-1350
www.ccourt.co.macon.il.us

Moultrie County
Cynthia J. Braden
10 South Main Street
Suite 7
Sullivan, IL 61951-1969
Phone: 217-728-4622
Fax: 217-728-7833
www.circuit-clerk.moultrie.
    il.us

Piatt County
Charles A. Barre
101 West Washington Street
Monticello, IL 61856-0288
Phone: 217-762-4966
Fax: 217-762-8394

Seventh Judicial Circuit

Greene County
V. "Tunie" Brannan
519 North Main Street
Carrollton, IL 62016-1093
Phone: 217-942-3421
Fax: 217-942-5431

Jersey County
Charles E. Huebener
201 West Pearl
Jerseyville, IL 62052-1852
Phone: 618-498-5571
Fax: 618-498-6128

Macoupin County
Mike Mathis
201 East Main Street
Carlinville, IL 62626-1824
Phone: 217-854-3211
Fax: 217-854-7361

Morgan County
Theresa Lonergan
300 West State Street
Box 1120
Jacksonville, IL 62650-1165
Phone: 217-243-5419
Fax: 217-243-2009

Sangamon County
Anthony P. Libri
200 South 9th Street
Room 405
Springfield, IL 62701-1299
Phone: 217-753-6674
Fax: 217-753-6665
www.sangamoncounty
    circuitclerk.org
www.co.sangamon.il.us/court/
    default.htm

Scott County
Joni Garrett
35 East Market Street
Winchester, IL 62694-1216
Phone: 217-742-5217
Fax: 217-742-5853

Eighth Judicial Circuit

Adams County
Randy Frese
521 Vermont Street
Quincy, IL 62301-2934
Phone: 217-277-2100
Fax: 217-277-2116
www.co.adams.il.us/circuit_
    clerk/index.htm

Brown County
Doris Todd
#1 Court Street
Mt. Sterling, IL 62353-1233
Phone: 217-773-2713
Fax: 217-773-2433

Calhoun County
Yvonne Macauley
Main and County Roads
Hardin, IL 62047-0486
Phone: 618-576-2451
Fax: 618-576-9541

Cass County
Evelyn K. Trenter
P.O. Box 203
Virginia, IL 62691-0203
Phone: 217-452-7225
Fax: 217-452-7219

Mason County
Brenda Miller
125 North Plum
Havana, IL 62644-0377
Phone: 309-543-6619
Fax: 309-543-4214

Menard County
Penny Hoke
P.O. Box 466
Petersburg, IL 62675-0466
Phone: 217-632-2615
Fax: 217-632-4124

Pike County
Debbie Dugan
100 East Washington
Pittsfield, IL 62363-1497
Phone: 217-285-6612
Fax: 217-285-4726

Schuyler County
Elaine Boyd
Lafayette and Congress
P.O. Box 80
Rushville, IL 62681-0189
Phone: 217-322-4633
Fax: 217-322-6164

Ninth Judicial Circuit

Fulton County
Mary C. Hampton
100 North Main Street
P.O. Box 152
Lewistown, IL 61542-0152
Phone: 309-547-3041
Fax: 309-547-3674

Hancock County
John Neally
Courthouse Square
Box 189
Carthage, IL 62321 0189
Phone: 217-357-2616
Fax: 217-357-2231

Henderson County
Sandra D. Keane
4th and Warren
Box 546
Oquawka, IL 61469-0546
Phone: 309-867-3121
Fax: 309-867-3207

Knox County
Kelly A. Cheesman
200 South Cherry Street
Galesburg, IL 61401-4912
Phone: 309-343-3121
Fax: 309-343-0098

McDonough County
Kimberly Wilson
#1 Courthouse Square
P.O. Box 348
Macomb, IL 61455-0348
Phone: 309-837-4889
Fax: 309-833-4493

Warren County
Jill M. Morris
100 West Broadway
Monmouth, IL 61462-1795
Phone: 309-734-5179
Fax: 309-734-4151

Tenth Judicial Circuit

Marshall County
Gina M. Noe
122 North Prairie
P.O. Box 328
Lacon, IL 61540-0328
Phone: 309-246-6435
Fax: 309-246-2173

Peoria County
Robert Spears
324 Main Street
Room G22
Peoria, IL 61602-1319
Phone: 309-672-6989
Fax: 309-672-6228
www.co.peoria.il.us

Putnam County
Cathy J. Oliveri
120 North 4th Street
Hennepin, IL 61327-0207
Phone: 815-925-7016
Fax: 815-925-7492

Stark County
Marian E. Purtscher
130 Main Strcct
Box 426
Toulon, IL 61483 0120
Phone: 309-286-5941
Fax: 309-286-4039

Tazewell County
Pamela J. Gardner
342 Court Street
Pekin, IL 61554
Phone: 309-477-2214
Fax: 309-353-7801

Eleventh Judicial Circuit

Ford County
Kamalen K. Johnson
200 West State
Box 80
Paxton, IL 60957-0080
Phone: 217-379-2641
Fax: 217-379-3445

Livingston County
Judith K. Cremer
112 West Madison Street
Pontiac, IL 61764-0320
Phone: 815-844-2602
Fax: 815-844-2322

Logan County
Carla Bender
601 Broadway
P.O. Box 158
Lincoln, IL 62656-0158
Phone: 217-735-2376
Fax: 217-732-1231
www.co.logan.il.us

McLean County
Sandra K. Parker
104 West Front Street
Room 404
Bloomington, IL 61702-2400
Phone: 309-888-5324
Fax: 309-888-5281
www.co.mclean.il.us/circuitclerk

Woodford County
Carol J. Newtson
115 North Main Street
P.O. Box 284
Eureka, IL 61530-0284
Phone: 309-467-3312
Fax: 309-467-7377

Twelfth Judicial Circuit

Will County
Pamela J. McGuire
14 West Jefferson Street
Suite 212
Joliet, IL 60432-4399
Phone: 815-727-8585
Fax: 815-727-8896
www.willcountycircuitcourt.com

Thirteenth Judicial Circuit

Bureau County
Michael L. Miroux
700 South Main Street
Princeton, IL 61356-2037
Phone: 815-872-2001
Fax: 815-872-0027
www.bccirclk.gov

Grundy County
Karen Slattery
111 East Washington Street
Room 30
Morris, IL 60450-0707
Phone: 815-941-3258
Fax: 815-941-3265

LaSalle County

Joseph Carey
119 West Madison
Ottawa, IL 61350-0617
Phone: 815 434 8671
Fax: 815-433-9198
www.lasallecounty.com

Fourteenth Judicial Circuit

Henry County

Debra J. Doss
307 West Center Street
Cambridge, IL 61238
Phone: 309-937-3572
Fax: 309-937-3990

Mercer County

Jeff Benson
100 Southeast 3rd Street
P.O. Box 175
Aledo, IL 61231-0175
Phone: 309-582-7122
Fax: 309-582-7121

Rock Island County

Lisa L. Bierman
210 15th Street
Box 5230
Rock Island, IL 61201-5230
Phone: 309-786-4451
Fax: 309-786-3029

Whiteside County

Sheila Schipper
200 East Knox Street
Morrison, IL 61270-2819
Phone: 815-772-5188
Fax: 815-772-5187
www.whiteside.org/Cntyclerk/
cntyclerk.html

Fifteenth Judicial Circuit

Carroll County

Sherri A. Miller
301 North Main Street
Mt. Carroll, IL 61053-0032
Phone: 815-244-0230
Fax: 815-244-3869

Jo Daviess County

Sharon A. Wand
330 North Bench Street
Galena, IL 61036-1828
Phone: 815-777-0037
Fax: 815-776-9146

Lee County

Denise A. McCaffrey
309 South Galena
Box 325
Dixon, IL 61021-0325
Phone: 815-284-5234
Fax: 815-288-5615

Ogle County

Martin W. Typer
106 South 5th
Suite 300
Oregon, IL 61061-0337
Phone: 815-732-3201
Fax: 815-732-6273
www.oglecounty.org/marty/
circuitclerk.html

Stephenson County

Bonnie K. Curran
15 North Galena Street
Freeport, IL 61032-0785
Phone: 815-235-8266
Fax: 815-233-1576
www.co.stephenson.il.us/
circuitclerk

Sixteenth Judicial Circuit

DeKalb County

Maureen Josh
133 West State Street
Sycamore, IL 60178-1416
Phone: 815-895-7131
Fax: 815-895-7140
www.circuitclerk.org

Kane County

Deborah Seyller
540 South Randall Road
St. Charles, IL 60174
Phone: 630-232-3413
Fax: 630-208-2172
www.cic.co.kane.il.us
www.co.kane.il.us/judicial/
    index.htm

Kendall County

Becky Morganegg
807 West John Street
P.O. Box M
Yorkville, IL 60560-0259
Phone: 630-553-4183
Fax: 630-553-4964

Seventeenth Judicial Circuit

Boone County

Nora Ohlsen
601 North Main
#303
Belvidere, IL 61008-2644
Phone: 815-544-0371
Fax: 815-547-9213
www.boonecountyil.org/
    circuitclerk/circuit.htm

Winnebago County

Marc A. Gasparini
400 West State Street
Rockford, IL 61101-1221
Phone: 815-987-5464
Fax: 815-987-3012
www.co.winnebago.il.us/
    Elected_Officials/Circuit_
    Clerk.htm
www.cc.co.winnebago.il.us

Eighteenth Judicial Circuit

DuPage County

Chris Kachiroubas
505 North County Farm Road
Wheaton, IL 60189-0707
Phone: 630-407-8700
Fax: 630-407-8575
www.co.dupage.il.us/
    courtclerk/index.cfm

Nineteenth Judicial Circuit

www.19thcircuitcourt.state.il.us

Lake County

Sally D. Coffelt
18 North County Street
Waukegan, IL 60085-4340
Phone: 847-377-3380
Fax: 847-360-6409
www.co.lake.il.us/circlk

McHenry County

Vernon W. Kays
2200 North Seminary Avenue
Woodstock, IL 60098-2837
Phone: 815-334-4000
Fax: 815-338-8583
www.co.mchenry.il.us/
    countydpt/circuit

Twentieth Judicial Circuit

Monroe County
Aaron Reitz
100 South Main Street
Room 115
Waterloo, IL 62298-1322
Phone: 618-939-8681
Fax: 618-939-1929

Perry County
Kim Kellerman
Courthouse Square
Box 219
Pinckneyville, IL 62274-0219
Phone: 618-357-6726
Fax: 618-357-8336

Randolph County
Barbara Brown
#1 Taylor Street
Room 302
Chester, IL 62233-0329
Phone: 618-826-3116
Fax: 618-826-3761

St. Clair County
C. Barney Metz
10 Public Square
Belleville, IL 62220-1623
Phone: 618-277-6832
Fax: 618-277-1562

Washington County
Carol Heggemeier
101 East Saint Louis Street
Nashville, IL 62263-1100
Phone: 618-327-4800
Fax: 618-327-3583

Twenty-First Judicial Circuit

Iroquois County
Arlene J. Hines
550 South Tenth Street
Watseka, IL 60970-1810
Phone: 815-432-6950
Fax: 815-432-0347

Kankakee County
Kathryn Thomas
450 East Court Street
Kankakee, IL 60901-3917
Phone: 815-937-2905
Fax: 815-939-8830

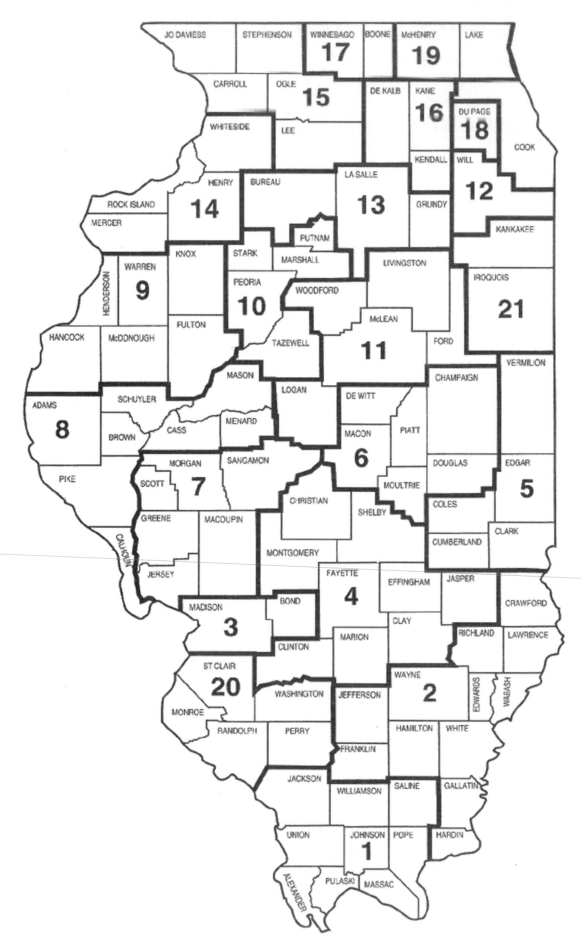

Illinois Statutes

This appendix contains selected portions of Chapter 750 of the Illinois Compiled Statutes, which govern the issue of divorce, and Section 1408 of the Uniformed Services Former Spouse's Protection Act. For a complete understanding and to review the other laws, visit your public library, local law library, or review Illinois laws on the Internet.

750 ILCS 5/401—This law shows the grounds for divorce.

Sec. 401. Dissolution of marriage.

(a) The court shall enter a judgment of dissolution of marriage if at the time the action was commenced one of the spouses was a resident of this State or was stationed in this State while a member of the armed services, and the residence or military presence had been maintained for 90 days next preceding the commencement of the action or the making of the finding; provided, however, that a finding of residence of a party in any judgment entered under this Act from January 1, 1982 through June 30, 1982 shall satisfy the former domicile requirements of this Act; and if one of the following grounds for dissolution has been proved:

(1) That, without cause or provocation by the petitioner: the respondent was at the time of such marriage, and continues to be naturally impotent; the respondent had a wife or husband living at the time of the marriage; the respon-

dent had committed adultery subsequent to the marriage; the respondent has wilfully deserted or absented himself or herself from the petitioner for the space of one year, including any period during which litigation may have pended between the spouses for dissolution of marriage or legal separation; the respondent has been guilty of habitual drunkenness for the space of 2 years; the respondent has been guilty of gross and confirmed habits caused by the excessive use of addictive drugs for the space of 2 years, or has attempted the life of the other by poison or other means showing malice, or has been guilty of extreme and repeated physical or mental cruelty, or has been convicted of a felony or other infamous crime; or the respondent has infected the other with a sexually transmitted disease. "Excessive use of addictive drugs", as used in this Section, refers to use of an addictive drug by a person when using the drug becomes a controlling or a dominant purpose of his life; or

(2) That the spouses have lived separate and apart for a continuous period in excess of 2 years and irreconcilable differences have caused the irretrievable breakdown of the marriage and the court determines that efforts at reconciliation have failed or that future attempts at reconciliation would be impracticable and not in the best interests of the family. If the spouses have lived separate and apart for a continuous period of not less than 6 months next preceding the entry of the judgment dissolving the marriage, as evidenced by testimony or affidavits of the spouses, the requirement of living separate and apart for a continuous period in excess of 2 years may be waived upon written stipulation of both spouses filed with the court. At any time after the parties cease to cohabit, the following periods shall be included in the period of separation:

(A) any period of cohabitation during which the parties attempted in good faith to reconcile and participated in marriage counseling under the guidance of any of the following: a psychiatrist, a clinical psychologist, a clinical social worker, a marriage and family therapist, a person authorized to provide counseling in accordance with the prescriptions of any religious denomination, or a person regularly engaged in providing family or marriage counseling; and

(B) any period of cohabitation under written agreement of the parties to attempt to reconcile.

In computing the period during which the spouses have lived separate and apart for purposes of this Section, periods during which the spouses were living separate and apart prior to July 1, 1984 are included.

(b) Judgment shall not be entered unless, to the extent it has jurisdiction to do so, the court has considered, approved, reserved or made provision for child custody, the support of any child of the marriage entitled to support, the maintenance of either spouse and the disposition of property. The court may enter a judgment for dissolution that reserves any of these issues either upon (i) agreement of the parties, or (ii) motion of either party and a finding by the court that appropriate circumstances exist.

The death of a party subsequent to entry of a judgment for dissolution but before judgment on reserved issues shall not abate the proceedings.

If any provision of this Section or its application shall be adjudged unconstitutional or invalid for any reason by any court of competent jurisdiction, that judgment shall not impair, affect or invalidate any other provision or application of this Section, which shall remain in full force and effect.

750 ILCS 5/452—These are the requirements for a Simplified Divorce.

Sec. 452. Petition. The parties to a dissolution proceeding may file a joint petition for simplified dissolution if they certify that all of the following conditions exist when the proceeding is commenced:

(a) Neither party is dependent on the other party for support or each party is willing to waive the right to support; and the parties understand that consultation with attorneys may help them determine eligibility for spousal support.

(b) Either party has met the residency requirement of Section 401 of this Act.

(c) Irreconcilable differences have caused the irretrievable breakdown of the marriage and the parties have been separated 6 months or more and efforts at reconciliation have failed or future attempts at reconciliation would be impracticable and not in the best interests of the family.

(d) No children were born of the relationship of the parties or adopted by the parties during the marriage, and the wife,

to her knowledge, is not pregnant by the husband.

(e) The duration of the marriage does not exceed 8 years.

(f) Neither party has any interest in real property.

(g) The parties waive any rights to maintenance.

(h) The total fair market value of all marital property, after deducting all encumbrances, is less than $10,000, the combined gross annualized income from all sources is less than $35,000, and neither party has a gross annualized income from all sources in excess of $20,000.

(i) The parties have disclosed to each other all assets and their tax returns for all years of the marriage.

(j) The parties have executed a written agreement dividing all assets in excess of $100 in value and allocating responsibility for debts and liabilities between the parties.

750 ILCS 5/502—This law lists the terms that should be addressed in a Marital Settlement Agreement.

Sec. 502. Agreement.

(a) To promote amicable settlement of disputes between parties to a marriage attendant upon the dissolution of their marriage, the parties may enter into a written or oral agreement containing provisions for disposition of any property owned by either of them, maintenance of either of them and support, custody and visitation of their children.

(b) The terms of the agreement, except those providing for the support, custody and visitation of children, are binding upon the court unless it finds, after considering the economic circumstances of the parties and any other relevant evidence produced by the parties, on their own motion or on request of the court, that the agreement is unconscionable.

(c) If the court finds the agreement unconscionable, it may request the parties to submit a revised agreement or upon hearing, may make orders for the disposition of property, maintenance, child support and other matters.

(d) Unless the agreement provides to the contrary, its terms shall be set forth in the judgment, and the parties shall be ordered to perform under such terms, or if the agreement provides that its terms shall not be set forth in the judgment, the judgment shall identify the agreement and state that the court has approved its terms.

(e) Terms of the agreement set forth in the judgment are enforceable by all remedies available for enforcement of a judgment, including contempt, and are enforceable as contract terms.

(f) Except for terms concerning the support, custody or visitation of children, the judgment may expressly preclude or limit modification of terms set forth in the judgment if the agreement so provides. Otherwise, terms of an agreement set forth in the judgment are automatically modified by modification of the judgment.

750 ILCS 5/504—These are the factors considered in awarding maintenance by law.

Sec. 504. Maintenance.

(a) In a proceeding for dissolution of marriage or legal separation or declaration of invalidity of marriage, or a proceeding for maintenance following dissolution of the marriage by a court which lacked personal jurisdiction over the absent spouse, the court may grant a temporary or permanent maintenance award for either spouse in amounts and for periods of time as the court deems just, without regard to marital misconduct, in gross or for fixed or indefinite periods of time, and the maintenance may be paid from the income or property of the other spouse after consideration of all relevant factors, including:

(1) the income and property of each party, including marital property apportioned and non-marital property assigned to the party seeking maintenance;

(2) the needs of each party;

(3) the present and future earning capacity of each party;

(4) any impairment of the present and future earning capacity of the party seeking maintenance due to that party devoting time to domestic duties or having forgone or delayed education, training, employment, or career opportunities due to the marriage;

(5) the time necessary to enable the party seeking maintenance to acquire appropriate education, training, and employment, and whether that party is able to support himself or herself through appropriate employment or is the custodian of a child making it appropriate that the custodian not seek employment;

(6) the standard of living established during the marriage;

(7) the duration of the marriage;

(8) the age and the physical and emotional condition of both parties;

(9) the tax consequences of the property division upon the respective economic circumstances of the parties;

(10) contributions and services by the party seeking maintenance to the education, training, career or career potential, or license of the other spouse;

(11) any valid agreement of the parties; and

(12) any other factor that the court expressly finds to be just and equitable.

(b) (Blank).

(b-5) Any maintenance obligation including any unallocated maintenance and child support obligation, or any portion of any support obligation, that becomes due and remains unpaid shall accrue simple interest as set forth in Section 505 of this Act.

(b-7) Any new or existing maintenance order including any unallocated maintenance and child support order entered by the court under this Section shall be deemed to be a series of judgments against the person obligated to pay support thereunder. Each such judgment to be in the amount of each payment or installment of support and each such judgment to be deemed entered as of the date the corresponding payment or installment becomes due under the terms of the support order, except no judgment shall arise as to any installment coming due after the termination of maintenance as provided by Section 510 of the Illinois Marriage and Dissolution of Marriage Act or the provisions of any order for maintenance. Each such judgment shall have the full force, effect and attributes of any other judgment of this State, including the ability to be enforced. A lien arises by operation of law against the real and personal property of the obligor for each installment of overdue support owed by the obligor.

(c) The court may grant and enforce the payment of maintenance during the pendency of an appeal as the court shall deem reasonable and proper.

(d) No maintenance shall accrue during the period in which a party is imprisoned for failure to comply with the court's order for the payment of such maintenance.

(e) When maintenance is to be paid through the clerk of the court in a county of 1,000,000 inhabitants or less, the order shall direct the obligor to pay to the clerk, in addition to the maintenance payments, all fees imposed by the county board under paragraph (3) of subsection (u) of Section 27.1 of the Clerks of Courts Act. Unless paid in cash or pursuant to an order for withholding, the payment of the fee shall be by a separate instrument from the support payment and shall be made to the order of the Clerk.

750 ILCS 5/505—This is the most important part of the law on calculating child support.

Sec. 505. Child support; contempt; penalties.

(a) In a proceeding for dissolution of marriage, legal separation, declaration of invalidity of marriage, a proceeding for child support following dissolution of the marriage by a court which lacked personal jurisdiction over the absent spouse, a proceeding for modification of a previous order for child support under Section 510 of this Act, or any proceeding authorized under Section 501 or 601 of this Act, the court may order either or both parents owing a duty of support to a child of the marriage to pay an amount reasonable and necessary for his support, without regard to marital misconduct. The duty of support owed to a child includes the obligation to provide for the reasonable and necessary physical, mental and emotional health needs of the child. For purposes of this Section, the term "child" shall include any child under age 18 and any child under age 19 who is still attending high school.

(1) The Court shall determine the minimum amount of support by using the following guidelines:

Number of Children	Percent of Supporting Party's Net Income
1	20%
2	28%
3	32%
4	40%
5	45%
6 or more	50%

(2) The above guidelines shall be applied in each case unless the court makes a finding that application of the guidelines would be inappropriate, after considering the best interests of the child in light of evidence including but not limited to one or more of the following relevant factors:

(a) the financial resources and needs of the child;

(b) the financial resources and needs of the custodial parent;

(c) the standard of living the child would have enjoyed had the marriage not been dissolved;

(d) the physical and emotional condition of the child, and his educational needs; and

(e) the financial resources and needs of the non-custodial parent. If the court deviates from the guidelines, the court's finding shall state the amount of support that would have been required under the guidelines, if determinable. The court shall include the reason or reasons for the variance from the guidelines.

(3) "Net income" is defined as the total of all income from all sources, minus the following deductions:

(a) Federal income tax (properly calculated withholding or estimated payments);

(b) State income tax (properly calculated withholding or estimated payments);

(c) Social Security (FICA payments);

(d) Mandatory retirement contributions required by law or as a condition of employment;

(e) Union dues;

(f) Dependent and individual health/hospitalization insurance premiums;

(g) Prior obligations of support or maintenance actually paid pursuant to a court order;

(h) Expenditures for repayment of debts that represent reasonable and necessary expenses for the production of income, medical expenditures necessary to preserve life or health, reasonable expenditures for the benefit of the child and the other parent, exclusive of gifts. The court shall reduce net income in determining the minimum amount of support to be ordered only for the period that such payments are due and shall enter an order containing provisions for its self-executing modification upon termination of such payment period.

(4) In cases where the court order provides for health/hospitalization insurance coverage pursuant to Section 505.2 of this Act, the premiums for that insurance, or that portion of the premiums for which the supporting party is responsible in the case of insurance provided through an employer's health insurance plan where the employer pays a portion of the premiums, shall be subtracted from net income in determining the minimum amount of support to be ordered.

750 ILCS 5/602.1—This law addresses the issue of custody.

Sec. 602.1.

(a) The dissolution of marriage, the declaration of invalidity of marriage, the legal separation of the parents, or the parents living separate and apart shall not diminish parental powers, rights, and responsibilities except as the court for good reason may determine under the standards of Section 602.

(b) Upon the application of either or both parents, or upon its own motion, the court shall consider an award of joint custody. Joint custody means custody determined pursuant to a Joint Parenting Agreement or a Joint Parenting Order. In such cases, the court shall initially request the parents to produce a Joint Parenting Agreement. Such Agreement shall specify each parent's powers, rights and responsibilities for the personal care of the child and for major decisions such as education, health care, and religious training. The Agreement shall further specify a procedure by which proposed changes, disputes and alleged breaches may be mediated or otherwise

resolved and shall provide for a periodic review of its terms by the parents. In producing a Joint Parenting Agreement, the parents shall be flexible in arriving at resolutions which further the policy of this State as expressed in Sections 102 and 602. For the purpose of assisting the court in making a determination whether an award of joint custody is appropriate, the court may order mediation and may direct that an investigation be conducted pursuant to the provisions of Section 605. If there is a danger to the health or safety of a partner, joint mediation shall not be required by the court. In the event the parents fail to produce a Joint Parenting Agreement, the court may enter an appropriate Joint Parenting Order under the standards of Section 602 which shall specify and contain the same elements as a Joint Parenting Agreement, or it may award sole custody under the standards of Sections 602, 607, and 608.

(c) The court may enter an order of joint custody if it determines that joint custody would be in the best interests of the child, taking into account the following:

(1) the ability of the parents to cooperate effectively and consistently in matters that directly affect the joint parenting of the child. "Ability of the parents to cooperate" means the parents' capacity to substantially comply with a Joint Parenting Order. The court shall not consider the inability of the parents to cooperate effectively and consistently in matters that do not directly affect the joint parenting of the child;

(2) The residential circumstances of each parent; and

(3) all other factors which may be relevant to the best interest of the child.

(d) Nothing within this section shall imply or presume that joint custody shall necessarily mean equal parenting time. The physical residence of the child in joint custodial situations shall be determined by:

(1) express agreement of the parties; or

(2) order of the court under the standards of this Section.

(e) Notwithstanding any other provision of law, access to records and information pertaining to a child, including but not limited to medical, dental, child care and school records, shall not be denied to a parent for the reason that such parent is not the child's custodial parent; however, no parent shall have access to the school records of a child if the parent is prohibited by an order of protection from inspecting or obtaining such records pursuant to the Illinois Domestic Violence Act of 1986, as now or hereafter amended.

750 ILCS 5/607—The following two laws are on the topic of visitation. This includes both parent, grandparent, sibling, and other interested parities who wish to get a court order for visitation.

Sec. 607. Visitation.

(a) A parent not granted custody of the child is entitled to reasonable visitation rights unless the court finds, after a hearing, that visitation would endanger seriously the child's physical, mental, moral or emotional health. If the custodian's street address is not identified, pursuant to Section 708, the court shall require the parties to identify reasonable alternative arrangements for visitation by a non-custodial parent, including but not limited to visitation of the minor child at the residence of another person or at a local public or private facility.

(a-3) Nothing in subsection (a-5) of this Section shall apply to a child in whose interests a petition under Section 2-13 of the Juvenile Court Act of 1987 is pending.

(a-5) (1) Except as otherwise provided in this subsection (a-5), any grandparent, great-grandparent, or sibling may file a petition for visitation rights to a minor child if there is an unreasonable denial of visitation by a parent and at least one of the following conditions exists:

(A) one parent of the child is incompetent as a matter of law or deceased or has been sentenced to a period of imprisonment for more than 1 year;

(B) the child's mother and father are divorced or have been legally separated from each other during the 3 month period prior to the filing of the petition and at least one parent does not object to the grandparent, great-grandparent, or sibling having visitation with the child. The visitation of the grandparent, great-grandparent, or sibling must not diminish the visitation of the parent who is not related to the grandparent, great-grandparent, or sibling seeking visitation;

(C) the court, other than a Juvenile Court, has terminated a parent-child relationship and the grandparent, great-grandparent, or sibling is the parent of the person whose parental rights have been terminated, except in cases of adoption. The visitation must not be used to allow the parent who lost parental rights to unlawfully visit with the child;

(D) the child is born out of wedlock, the parents are not living together, and the petitioner is a maternal grandparent, great-grandparent, or sibling of the child born out of wedlock; or

(E) the child is born out of wedlock, the parents are not living together, the petitioner is a paternal grandparent, great-grandparent, or sibling, and the paternity has been established by a court of competent jurisdiction.

(2) The grandparent, great-grandparent, or sibling of a parent whose parental rights have been terminated through an adoption proceeding may not petition for visitation rights.

(3) In making a determination under this subsection (a-5), there is a rebuttable presumption that a fit parent's actions and decisions regarding grandparent, great-grandparent, or sibling visitation are not harmful to the child's mental, physical, or emotional health. The burden is on the party filing a petition under this Section to prove that the parent's actions and decisions regarding visitation times are harmful to the child's mental, physical, or emotional health.

(4) In determining whether to grant visitation, the court shall consider the following:

(A) the preference of the child if the child is determined to be of sufficient maturity to express a preference;

(B) the mental and physical health of the child;

(C) the mental and physical health of the grandparent, great-grandparent, or sibling;

(D) the length and quality of the prior relationship between the child and the grandparent, great-grandparent, or sibling;

(E) the good faith of the party in filing the petition;

(F) the good faith of the person denying visitation;

(G) the quantity of the visitation time requested and the potential adverse impact that visitation would have on the child's customary activities;

(H) whether the child resided with the petitioner for at least 6 consecutive months with or without the current custodian present;

(I) whether the petitioner had frequent or regular contact with the child for at least 12 consecutive months; and

(J) any other fact that establishes that the loss of the relationship between the petitioner and the child is likely to harm the child's mental, physical, or emotional health.

(5) The court may order visitation rights for the grandparent, great-grandparent, or sibling that include reasonable access without requiring overnight or possessory visitation.

(a-7) (1) Unless by stipulation of the parties, no motion to modify a grandparent, great-grandparent, or sibling visitation order may be made earlier than 2 years after the date the order was filed, unless the court permits it to be made on the basis of affidavits that there is reason to believe the child's present environment may endanger seriously the child's mental, physical, or emotional health.

(2) The court shall not modify a prior grandparent, great-grandparent, or sibling visitation order unless it finds by clear and convincing evidence, upon the basis of facts that have arisen since the prior visitation order or that were unknown to the court at the time of entry of the prior visitation, that a change has occurred in the circumstances of the child or his or her custodian, and that the modification is necessary to protect the mental, physical, or emotional health of the child. The court shall state in its decision specific findings of fact in support of its modification or termination of the grandparent, great-grandparent, or sibling visitation.

(3) Attorney fees and costs shall be assessed against a party seeking modification of the visitation order if the court finds that the modification action is vexatious and constitutes harassment.

(4) Notice under this subsection (a-7) shall be given as provided in subsections (c) and (d) of Section 601.

(b)(1) (Blank.)

(1.5) The Court may grant reasonable visitation privileges to a stepparent upon petition to the court by the stepparent, with notice to the parties required to be notified under Section 601 of this Act, if the court determines that it is in the best interests and welfare of the child, and may issue any necessary orders to enforce those visitation privileges. A petition for visitation privileges may be filed under this paragraph (1.5) whether or not a petition pursuant to this Act has been previously filed or is currently pending if the following circumstances are met:

(A) the child is at least 12 years old;

(B) the child resided continuously with the parent and stepparent for at least 5 years;

(C) the parent is deceased or is disabled and is unable to care for the child;

(D) the child wishes to have reasonable visitation with the stepparent; and

(E) the stepparent was providing for the care, control, and welfare to the child prior to the initiation of the petition for visitation.

(2)(A) A petition for visitation privileges shall not be filed pursuant to this subsection (b) by the parents or grandparents of a putative father if the paternity of the putative father has not been legally established.

(B) A petition for visitation privileges may not be filed under this subsection (b) if the child who is the subject of the grandparents' or great-grandparents' petition has been voluntarily surrendered by the parent or parents, except for a surrender to the Illinois Department of Children and Family Services or a foster care facility, or has been previously adopted by an individual or individuals who are not related to the biological parents of the child or is the subject of a pending adoption petition by an individual or individuals who are not related to the biological parents of the child.

(3) (Blank).

(c) The court may modify an order granting or denying visitation rights of a parent whenever modification would serve the best interest of the child; but the court shall not restrict a parent's visitation rights unless it finds that the visitation would endanger seriously the child's physical, mental, moral or emotional health. The court may modify an order granting, denying, or limiting visitation rights of a grandparent, great-grandparent, or sibling of any minor child whenever a change of circumstances has occurred based on facts occurring subsequent to the judgment and the court finds by clear and convincing evidence that the modification is in the best interest of the minor child.

(d) If any court has entered an order prohibiting a non-custodial parent of a child from any contact with a child or restricting the non-custodial parent's contact with the child, the following provisions shall apply:

(1) If an order has been entered granting visitation privileges with the child to a grandparent or great-grandparent who is related to the child through the non-custodial parent, the visitation privileges of the grandparent or great-grandparent may be revoked if:

(i) a court has entered an order prohibiting the non-custodial parent from any contact with the child, and the grandparent or great-grandparent is found to have used his or her visitation privileges to facilitate contact between the child and the non-custodial parent; or

(ii) a court has entered an order restricting the non-custodial parent's contact with the child, and the grandparent or great-grandparent is found to have used his or her visitation privileges to facilitate contact between the child and the non-custodial parent in a manner that violates the terms of the order restricting the non-custodial parent's contact with the child.

Nothing in this subdivision (1) limits the authority of the court to enforce its orders in any manner permitted by law.

(2) Any order granting visitation privileges with the child to a grandparent or great-grandparent who is related to the child through the non-custodial parent shall contain the following provision:

"If the (grandparent or great-grandparent, whichever is applicable) who has been granted visitation privileges under this order uses the visitation privileges to facilitate contact between the child and the child's non-custodial parent, the visitation privileges granted under this order shall be permanently revoked."

(e) No parent, not granted custody of the child, or grandparent, or great-grandparent, or stepparent, or sibling of any minor child, convicted of any offense involving an illegal sex act perpetrated upon a victim less than 18 years of age including but not limited to offenses for violations of Article 12 of the Criminal Code of 1961, is entitled to visitation rights while incarcerated or while on parole, probation, conditional discharge, periodic imprisonment, or mandatory supervised release for that offense, and upon discharge from incarceration for a misdemeanor offense or upon discharge from parole, probation, conditional discharge, periodic imprisonment, or mandatory supervised release for a felony offense, visitation shall be denied until the person successfully completes a treatment program approved by the court.

(f) Unless the court determines, after considering all relevant factors, including but not limited to those set forth in Section 602(a), that it would be in the best interests of the child to allow visitation, the court shall not enter an order providing visitation rights and pursuant to a motion to modify visitation shall revoke visitation rights previously granted to any person who would otherwise be entitled to petition for visitation rights under this Section who has been convicted of first degree murder of the parent, grandparent, great-grandparent, or sibling of the child who is the subject of the order. Until an order is entered pursuant to this subsection, no person shall visit, with the child present, a person who has been convicted of first degree murder of the parent, grandparent, great-grandparent, or sibling of the child without the consent of the child's parent, other than a parent convicted of first degree murder as set forth herein, or legal guardian.

(g) If an order has been entered limiting, for cause, a minor child's contact or visitation with a grandparent, great-grandparent, or sibling on the grounds that it was in the best interest of the child to do so, that order may be modified only upon a showing of a substantial change in circumstances occurring subsequent to the entry of the order with proof by clear and convincing evidence that modification is in the best interest of the minor child.

Sec. 607.1. Enforcement of visitation orders; visitation abuse.

(a) The circuit court shall provide an expedited procedure for enforcement of court ordered visitation in cases of visitation abuse. Visitation abuse occurs when a party has willfully and without justification: (1) denied another party visitation as set forth by the court; or (2) exercised his or her visitation rights in a manner that is harmful to the child or child's custodian.

(b) An Action may be commenced by filing a petition setting forth: (i) the petitioner's name, residence address or mailing address, and telephone number; (ii) respondent's name and place of residence, place of employment, or mailing address; (iii) the nature of the visitation abuse, giving dates and other relevant information; (iv) that a reasonable attempt was made to resolve the dispute; and (v) the relief sought.

Notice of the filing of the petitions shall be given as provided in Section 511.

(c) After hearing all of the evidence, the court may order one or more of the following:

(1) Modification of the visitation order to specifically outline periods of visitation or restrict visitation as provided by law.

(2) Supervised visitation with a third party or public agency.

(3) Make up visitation of the same time period, such as weekend for weekend, holiday for holiday.

(4) Counseling or mediation, except in cases where there is evidence of domestic violence, as defined in Section 1 of the Domestic Violence Shelters Act, occurring between the parties.

(5) Other appropriate relief deemed equitable.

(d) Nothing contained in this Section shall be construed to limit the court's contempt power, except as provided in subsection (g) of this Section.

(e) When the court issues an order holding a party in contempt of court for violation of a visitation order, the clerk shall transmit a copy of the contempt order to the sheriff of the county. The sheriff shall furnish a copy of each contempt order to the Department of State Police on a daily basis in the form and manner required by the Department. The Department shall maintain a complete record and index of the contempt orders and make this data available to all local law enforcement agencies.

(f) Attorney fees and costs shall be assessed against a party if the court finds that the enforcement action is vexatious and constitutes harassment.

(g) A person convicted of unlawful visitation interference under Section 10-5.5 of the Criminal Code of 1961 shall not be subject to the provisions of this Section and the court may not enter a contempt order for visitation abuse against any person for the same conduct for which the person was convicted of unlawful visitation interference or subject that person to the sanctions provided for in this Section.

USFSPA—The following law applies to those in the military.
United States Code Title 10/Chapter 71/ § 1408. Payment of retired or retainer pay in compliance with court orders

(a) Definitions.— In this section:

(1) The term "court" means—

(A) any court of competent jurisdiction of any State, the District of Columbia, the Commonwealth of Puerto Rico, Guam, American Samoa, the Virgin Islands, the Northern Mariana Islands, and the Trust Territory of the Pacific Islands;

(B) any court of the United States (as defined in section 451 of title 28) having competent jurisdiction;

(C) any court of competent jurisdiction of a foreign country with which the United States has an agreement requiring the United States to honor any court order of such country; and

(D) any administrative or judicial tribunal of a State competent to enter orders for support or maintenance (including a State agency administering a program under a State plan approved under part D of title IV of the Social Security Act), and, for purposes of this subparagraph, the term "State" includes the District of Columbia, the Commonwealth of Puerto Rico, the Virgin Islands, Guam, and American Samoa.

(2) The term "court order" means a final decree of divorce, dissolution, annulment, or legal separation issued by a court, or a court ordered, ratified, or approved property settlement incident to such a decree (including a final decree modifying the terms of a previously issued decree of divorce, dissolution, annulment, or legal

separation, or a court ordered, ratified, or approved property settlement incident to such previously issued decree), or a support order, as defined in section 453(p) of the Social Security Act (42 U.S.C. 653 (p)), which—

(A) is issued in accordance with the laws of the jurisdiction of that court;

(B) provides for—

(i) payment of child support (as defined in section 459(i)(2) of the Social Security Act (42 U.S.C. 659 (i)(2)));

(ii) payment of alimony (as defined in section 459(i)(3) of the Social Security Act (42 U.S.C. 659 (i)(3))); or

(iii) division of property (including a division of community property); and

(C) in the case of a division of property, specifically provides for the payment of an amount, expressed in dollars or as a percentage of disposable retired pay, from the disposable retired pay of a member to the spouse or former spouse of that member.

(3) The term "final decree" means a decree from which no appeal may be taken or from which no appeal has been taken within the time allowed for taking such appeals under the laws applicable to such appeals, or a decree from which timely appeal has been taken and such appeal has been finally decided under the laws applicable to such appeals.

(4) The term "disposable retired pay" means the total monthly retired pay to which a member is entitled less amounts which—

(A) are owed by that member to the United States for previous overpayments of retired pay and for recoupments

required by law resulting from entitlement to retired pay;

(B) are deducted from the retired pay of such member as a result of forfeitures of retired pay ordered by a court-martial or as a result of a waiver of retired pay required by law in order to receive compensation under title 5 or title 38;

(C) in the case of a member entitled to retired pay under chapter 61 of this title, are equal to the amount of retired pay of the member under that chapter computed using the percentage of the member's disability on the date when the member was retired (or the date on which the member's name was placed on the temporary disability retired list); or

(D) are deducted because of an election under chapter 73 of this title to provide an annuity to a spouse or former spouse to whom payment of a portion of such member's retired pay is being made pursuant to a court order under this section.

(5) The term "member" includes a former member entitled to retired pay under section 12731 of this title.

(6) The term "spouse or former spouse" means the husband or wife, or former husband or wife, respectively, of a member who, on or before the date of a court order, was married to that member.

(7) The term "retired pay" includes retainer pay.

(b) Effective Service of Process.— For the purposes of this section—

(1) service of a court order is effective if—

(A) an appropriate agent of the Secretary concerned designated for receipt of service of court orders under regulations prescribed pursuant to subsection (i) or, if no agent has been so designated, the Secretary concerned, is personally served or is served by facsimile or electronic transmission or by mail;

(B) the court order is regular on its face;

(C) the court order or other documents served with the court order identify the member concerned and include, if possible, the social security number of such member; and

(D) the court order or other documents served with the court order certify that the rights of the member under the Soldiers' and Sailors' Civil Relief Act of 1940 (50 App. U.S.C. 501 et seq.) were observed; and

(2) a court order is regular on its face if the order—

(A) is issued by a court of competent jurisdiction;

(B) is legal in form; and

(C) includes nothing on its face that provides reasonable notice that it is issued without authority of law.

(c) Authority for Court To Treat Retired Pay as Property of the Member and Spouse.—

(1) Subject to the limitations of this section, a court may treat disposable retired pay payable to a member for pay periods beginning after June 25, 1981, either as property solely of the member or as property of the member and his spouse in accordance with the law of the jurisdiction of such court. A court may not treat retired pay as property in any proceeding to divide or partition any amount of retired pay of a member as the property of the member and the member's spouse or former spouse

if a final decree of divorce, dissolution, annulment, or legal separation (including a court ordered, ratified, or approved property settlement incident to such decree) affecting the member and the member's spouse or former spouse

(A) was issued before June 25, 1981, and

(B) did not treat (or reserve jurisdiction to treat) any amount of retired pay of the member as property of the member and the member's spouse or former spouse.

(2) Notwithstanding any other provision of law, this section does not create any right, title, or interest which can be sold, assigned, transferred, or otherwise disposed of (including by inheritance) by a spouse or former spouse. Payments by the Secretary concerned under subsection (d) to a spouse or former spouse with respect to a division of retired pay as the property of a member and the member's spouse under this subsection may not be treated as amounts received as retired pay for service in the uniformed services.

(3) This section does not authorize any court to order a member to apply for retirement or retire at a particular time in order to effectuate any payment under this section

(4) A court may not treat the disposable retired pay of a member in the manner described in paragraph (1) unless the court has jurisdiction over the member by reason of

(A) his residence, other than because of military assignment, in the territorial jurisdiction of the court,

(B) his domicile in the territorial jurisdiction of the court, or

(C) his consent to the jurisdiction of the court.

(d) Payments by Secretary Concerned to (or for Benefit of) Spouse or Former Spouse.—

(1) After effective service on the Secretary concerned of a court order providing for the payment of child support or alimony or, with respect to a division of property, specifically providing for the payment of an amount of the disposable retired pay from a member to the spouse or a former spouse of the member, the Secretary shall make payments (subject to the limitations of this section) from the disposable retired pay of the member to the spouse or former spouse (or for the benefit of such spouse or former spouse to a State disbursement unit established pursuant to section 454B of the Social Security Act or other public payee designated by a State, in accordance with part D of title IV of the Social Security Act, as directed by court order, or as otherwise directed in accordance with such part D) in an amount sufficient to satisfy the amount of child support and alimony set forth in the court order and, with respect to a division of property, in the amount of disposable retired pay specifically provided for in the court order. In the case of a spouse or former spouse who, pursuant to section 408(a)(3) of the Social Security Act (42 U.S.C. 608 (a)(4)), assigns to a State the rights of the spouse or former spouse to receive support, the Secretary concerned may make the child support payments referred to in the preceding sentence to that State in amounts consistent with that assignment of rights. In the case of a member entitled to receive retired pay on the date of the effective service of the court order, such payments shall begin not later than 90 days after the date of effective service. In the case of a member not entitled to receive retired pay on the date of the effective service of the court order, such payments shall begin not later than 90 days after the date on which the member first becomes entitled to receive retired pay.

(2) If the spouse or former spouse to whom payments are to be made under this section was not married to the member for a period of 10 years or more during which the member performed at least 10 years of service creditable in determining the member's eligibility for retired pay, payments may not be made under this section to the extent that they include an amount resulting from the treatment by the court under subsection (c) of disposable retired pay of the member as property of the member or property of the member and his spouse.

(3) Payments under this section shall not be made more frequently than once each month, and the Secretary concerned shall not be required to vary normal pay and disbursement cycles for retired pay in order to comply with a court order.

(4) Payments from the disposable retired pay of a member pursuant to this section shall terminate in accordance with the terms of the applicable court order, but not later than the date of the death of the member or the date of the death of the spouse or former spouse to whom payments are being made, whichever occurs first.

(5) If a court order described in paragraph (1) provides for a division of property (including a division of community property) in addition to an amount of child support or alimony or the payment of an amount of disposable retired pay as the result of the court's treatment of such pay under subsection (c) as property of the member and his spouse, the Secretary concerned shall pay (subject to the limitations of this section) from the disposable retired pay of the member to the spouse or former spouse of the member, any part of the amount payable to the spouse or former spouse under the division of property upon effective service of a final court order of garnishment of such amount from such retired pay.

(6) In the case of a court order for which effective service is made on the Secretary concerned on or after August 22, 1996, and which provides for payments from the disposable retired pay of a member to satisfy the amount of child support set forth in the order, the authority provided in paragraph (1) to make payments from the disposable retired pay of a member to satisfy the amount of child support set forth in a court order shall apply to payment of any amount of child support arrearages set forth in that order as well as to amounts of child support that currently become due.

(7)(A) The Secretary concerned may not accept service of a court order that is an out-of-State modification, or comply with the provisions of such a court order, unless the court issuing that order has jurisdiction in the manner specified in subsection (c)(4) over both the member and the spouse or former spouse involved.

(B) A court order shall be considered to be an out-of-State modification for purposes of this paragraph if the order—

(i) modifies a previous court order under this section upon which payments under this subsection are based; and

(ii) is issued by a court of a State other than the State of the court that issued the previous court order.

(c) Limitations.—

(1) The total amount of the disposable retired pay of a member payable under all court orders pursuant to subsection (c) may not exceed 50 percent of such disposable retired pay.

(2) In the event of effective service of more than one court order which provide for payment to a spouse and one or more former spouses or to more than one former spouse, the disposable retired pay of the member shall be used to satisfy (subject to the limitations of paragraph (1)) such court orders on a first-come, first-served basis. Such court orders shall be satisfied (subject to the limitations of paragraph (1)) out of that amount of disposable retired pay which remains after the satisfaction of all court orders which have been previously served.

(3)(A) In the event of effective service of conflicting court orders under this section which assert to direct that different amounts be paid during a month to the same spouse or former spouse of the same member, the Secretary concerned shall—

(i) pay to that spouse from the member's disposable retired pay the least amount directed to be paid during that month by any such conflicting court order, but not more than the amount of disposable retired pay which remains available for payment of such court orders based on when such court orders were effectively served and the limitations of paragraph (1) and subparagraph (B) of paragraph (4);

(ii) retain an amount of disposable retired pay that is equal to the lesser of—

(I) the difference between the largest amount required by any conflicting court order to be paid to the spouse or former spouse and the amount payable to the spouse or former spouse under clause (i); and

(II) the amount of disposable retired pay which remains available for payment of any conflicting court order based on when such court order was effectively served and the limitations of paragraph (1) and subparagraph (B) of paragraph (4); and

(iii) pay to that member the amount which is equal to the amount of that member's disposable retired pay (less any amount paid during such month pursuant to legal process served under section 459 of the Social Security Act (42 U.S.C. 659) and any amount paid during such month pursuant to court orders effectively served under this section, other than such conflicting court orders) minus—

(I) the amount of disposable retired pay paid under clause (i); and

(II) the amount of disposable retired pay retained under clause (ii).

(B) The Secretary concerned shall hold the amount retained under clause (ii) of subparagraph (A) until such time as that Secretary is provided with a court order which has been certified by the member and the spouse or former spouse to be

valid and applicable to the retained amount. Upon being provided with such an order, the Secretary shall pay the retained amount in accordance with the order.

(4)(A) In the event of effective service of a court order under this section and the service of legal process pursuant to section 459 of the Social Security Act (42 U.S.C. 659), both of which provide for payments during a month from the same member, satisfaction of such court orders and legal process from the retired pay of the member shall be on a first-come, first-served basis. Such court orders and legal process shall be satisfied out of moneys which are subject to such orders and legal process and which remain available in accordance with the limitations of paragraph (1) and subparagraph (B) of this paragraph during such month after the satisfaction of all court orders or legal process which have been previously served.

(B) Notwithstanding any other provision of law, the total amount of the disposable retired pay of a member payable by the Secretary concerned under all court orders pursuant to this section and all legal processes pursuant to section 459 of the Social Security Act (42 U.S.C. 659) with respect to a member may not exceed 65 percent of the amount of the retired pay payable to such member that is considered under section 462 of the Social Security Act (42 U.S.C. 662) to be remuneration for employment that is payable by the United States.

(5) A court order which itself or because of previously served court orders provides for the payment of an amount which exceeds the amount of disposable retired

pay available for payment because of the limit set forth in paragraph (1), or which, because of previously served court orders or legal process previously served under section 459 of the Social Security Act (42 U.S.C. 659), provides for payment of an amount that exceeds the maximum amount permitted under paragraph (1) or subparagraph (B) of paragraph (4), shall not be considered to be irregular on its face solely for that reason. However, such order shall be considered to be fully satisfied for purposes of this section by the payment to the spouse or former spouse of the maximum amount of disposable retired pay permitted under paragraph (1) and subparagraph (B) of paragraph (4).

(6) Nothing in this section shall be construed to relieve a member of liability for the payment of alimony, child support, or other payments required by a court order on the grounds that payments made out of disposable retired pay under this section have been made in the maximum amount permitted under paragraph (1) or subparagraph (B) of paragraph (4). Any such unsatisfied obligation of a member may be enforced by any means available under law other than the means provided under this section in any case in which the maximum amount permitted under paragraph (1) has been paid and under section 459 of the Social Security Act (42 U.S.C. 659) in any case in which the maximum amount permitted under subparagraph (B) of paragraph (4) has been paid.

(f) Immunity of Officers and Employees of United States.—

(1) The United States and any officer or employee of the United States shall not be liable with respect to any payment made from retired pay to any member, spouse, or former spouse pursuant to a court order that is regular on its face if such payment is made in accordance with this section and the regulations prescribed pursuant to subsection (i).

(2) An officer or employee of the United States who, under regulations prescribed pursuant to subsection (i), has the duty to respond to interrogatories shall not be subject under any law to any disciplinary action or civil or criminal liability or penalty for, or because of, any disclosure of information made by him in carrying out any of his duties which directly or indirectly pertain to answering such interrogatories.

(g) Notice to Member of Service of Court Order on Secretary Concerned.— A person receiving effective service of a court order under this section shall, as soon as possible, but not later than 30 days after the date on which effective service is made, send a written notice of such court order (together with a copy of such order) to the member affected by the court order at his last known address.

(h) Benefits for Dependents Who Are Victims of Abuse by Members Losing Right to Retired Pay.—

(1) If, in the case of a member or former member of the armed forces referred to in paragraph (2)(A), a court order provides (in the manner applicable to a division of property) for the payment of an amount from the disposable retired pay of that member or former member (as certified under paragraph (4)) to an eligible spouse or former spouse of that member or former

member, the Secretary concerned, beginning upon effective service of such court order, shall pay that amount in accordance with this subsection to such spouse or former spouse.

(2) A spouse or former spouse of a member or former member of the armed forces is eligible to receive payment under this subsection if—

(A) the member or former member, while a member of the armed forces and after becoming eligible to be retired from the armed forces on the basis of years of service, has eligibility to receive retired pay terminated as a result of misconduct while a member involving abuse of a spouse or dependent child (as defined in regulations prescribed by the Secretary of Defense or, for the Coast Guard when it is not operating as a service in the Navy, by the Secretary of Homeland Security); and

(B) the spouse or former spouse—

(i) was the victim of the abuse and was married to the member or former member at the time of that abuse; or

(ii) is a natural or adopted parent of a dependent child of the member or former member who was the victim of the abuse.

(3) The amount certified by the Secretary concerned under paragraph (4) with respect to a member or former member of the armed forces referred to in paragraph (2)(A) shall be deemed to be the disposable retired pay of that member or former member for the purposes of this subsection.

(4) Upon the request of a court or an eligible spouse or former spouse of a member or former member of the armed forces referred to in paragraph (2)(A) in connection with a civil action for the issuance of a court order in the case of that member or former member, the Secretary concerned shall determine and certify the amount of the monthly retired pay that the member or former member would have been entitled to receive as of the date of the certification—

(A) if the member or former member's eligibility for retired pay had not been terminated as described in paragraph (2)(A); and

(B) if, in the case of a member or former member not in receipt of retired pay immediately before that termination of eligibility for retired pay, the member or former member had retired on the effective date of that termination of eligibility.

(5) A court order under this subsection may provide that whenever retired pay is increased under section 1401a of this title (or any other provision of law), the amount payable under the court order to the spouse or former spouse of a member or former member described in paragraph (2)(A) shall be increased at the same time by the percent by which the retired pay of the member or former member would have been increased if the member or former member were receiving retired pay.

(6) Notwithstanding any other provision of law, a member or former member of the armed forces referred to in paragraph (2)(A) shall have no ownership interest in, or claim against, any amount payable under this section to a spouse or former spouse of the member or former member.

(7)(A) If a former spouse receiving payments under this subsection with respect to a member or former member referred to in paragraph (2)(A) marries again after such payments begin, the eligibility of the former spouse to receive further payments under this subsection shall terminate on the date of such marriage.

(B) A person's eligibility to receive payments under this subsection that is terminated under subparagraph (A) by reason of remarriage shall be resumed in the event of the termination of that marriage by the death of that person's spouse or by annulment or divorce. The resumption of payments shall begin as of the first day of the month in which that marriage is so terminated. The monthly amount of the payments shall be the amount that would have been paid if the continuity of the payments had not been interrupted by the marriage.

(8) Payments in accordance with this subsection shall be made out of funds in the Department of Defense Military Retirement Fund established by section 1461 of this title or, in the case of the Coast Guard, out of funds appropriated to the Department of Homeland Security for payment of retired pay for the Coast Guard.

(9)(A) A spouse or former spouse of a member or former member of the armed forces referred to in paragraph (2)(A), while receiving payments in accordance with this subsection, shall be entitled to receive medical and dental care, to use commissary and exchange stores, and to receive any other benefit that a spouse or a former spouse of a retired member of the armed forces is entitled to receive on the basis of being a spouse or former spouse, as the case may be, of a retired member of the

armed forces in the same manner as if the member or former member referred to in paragraph (2)(A) was entitled to retired pay.

(B) A dependent child of a member or former member referred to in paragraph (2)(A) who was a member of the household of the member or former member at the time of the misconduct described in paragraph (2)(A) shall be entitled to receive medical and dental care, to use commissary and exchange stores, and to have other benefits provided to dependents of retired members of the armed forces in the same manner as if the member or former member referred to in paragraph (2)(A) was entitled to retired pay.

(C) If a spouse or former spouse or a dependent child eligible or entitled to receive a particular benefit under this paragraph is eligible or entitled to receive that benefit under another provision of law, the eligibility or entitlement of that spouse or former spouse or dependent child to such benefit shall be determined under such other provision of law instead of this paragraph.

(10)(A) For purposes of this subsection, in the case of a member of the armed forces who has been sentenced by a court-martial to receive a punishment that will terminate the eligibility of that member to receive retired pay if executed, the eligibility of that member to receive retired pay may, as determined by the Secretary concerned, be considered terminated effective upon the approval of that sentence by the person acting under section 860 (c) of this title (article 60(c) of the Uniform Code of Military Justice).

(B) If each form of the punishment that would result in the termination of eligibility to receive retired pay is later remitted, set aside, or mitigated to a punishment that does not result in the termination of that eligibility, a payment of benefits to the eligible recipient under this subsection that is based on the punishment so vacated, set aside, or mitigated shall cease. The cessation of payments shall be effective as of the first day of the first month following the month in which the Secretary concerned notifies the recipient of such benefits in writing that payment of the benefits will cease. The recipient may not be required to repay the benefits received before that effective date (except to the extent necessary to recoup any amount that was erroneous when paid).

(11) In this subsection, the term "dependent child", with respect to a member or former member of the armed forces referred to in paragraph (2)(A), means an unmarried legitimate child, including an adopted child or a stepchild of the member or former member, who—

(A) is under 18 years of age;

(B) is incapable of self-support because of a mental or physical incapacity that existed before becoming 18 years of age and is dependent on the member or former member for over one-half of the child's support; or

(C) if enrolled in a full-time course of study in an institution of higher education recognized by the Secretary of Defense for the purposes of this subparagraph, is under 23 years of age and is dependent on the member or former member for over one-half of the child's support.

(i) Certification Date.— It is not necessary that the date of a certification of the authenticity or completeness of a copy of a court order for child support received by the Secretary concerned for the purposes of this section be recent in relation to the date of receipt by the Secretary.

(j) Regulations.—The Secretaries concerned shall prescribe uniform regulations for the administration of this section.

(k) Relationship to Other Laws.—In any case involving an order providing for payment of child support (as defined in section 459(i)(2) of the Social Security Act) by a member who has never been married to the other parent of the child, the provisions of this section shall not apply, and the case shall be subject to the provisions of section 459 of such Act.

Checklists and Worksheets

The following are checklists and worksheets that may be useful to you in preparing for a divorce, whether you are using an attorney or not. Make photocopies for use as practice and for the final information that you will bring to the first meeting with your attorney. You should always keep a copy of each for future use or in case you make a mistake.

CHECKLISTS AND WORKSHEETS

DIVORCE INFORMATION

YOUR NAME: _____

ADDRESS: _____

_____

PHONE NO.: _____   WORK PHONE NO.: _____

EMPLOYER: _____

_____

DATE OF BIRTH: _____

SPOUSE NAME: _____

ADDRESS: _____

_____

PHONE NO.: _____   WORK PHONE NO.: _____

EMPLOYER: _____

_____

DATE OF BIRTH: _____

SPOUSE'S ATTORNEY: _____

DATE OF MARRIAGE: ___/___/___   PLACE MARRIED: _____

MONTHLY INCOME

	YOURS:	SPOUSE'S:
Salary:	_____	_____
Overtime/Commission:	_____	_____
Bonus:	_____	_____
Pension/Retirement:	_____	_____
Trust/Annuity:	_____	_____
Interest/Dividends:	_____	_____
Unemployment:	_____	_____
Workers' Comp:	_____	_____
Public Aid/Food Stamps:	_____	_____
Social Security:	_____	_____
Disability:	_____	_____
Rental Income:	_____	_____
Investments/Business:	_____	_____
Other:	_____	_____

CHILDREN

Name	Date of Birth	Social Security No.

INSURANCE INFORMATION
(LIFE, HOME, HEALTH, AUTO)

Insurance Co.	Type of Insurance	Policy #	Premium Paid

DEBTS

Creditor	Yours/Spouse's	Monthly Payment	TOTAL

PROPERTY OWNED
(HOME, LAND, VEHICLES, BOATS, TRAILERS, COLLECTIBLES)

Description	Approx. Value	Owner

OTHER ASSETS
(SAVINGS ACCOUNTS, CHECKING ACCOUNTS, CDS, INVESTMENTS)

Description	Approx. Value	Owner

STANDARD MONTHLY EXPENSES
(RENT, UTILITIES, TUITION, ETC.)

Creditor	Type of Expense	Monthly Payment

CHILD SUPPORT CALCULATION METHOD

Actual Monthly Gross Income from all sources $_____

Deductions (Monthly):

    a)   Federal Income Tax $_____

    b)   State Income Tax $_____

    c)   FICA (Social Security) $_____

    d)   Mandatory (not voluntary) pension/retirement
             contributions $_____

    e)   Union dues $_____

    f)   Health/hospitalization insurance premiums
             (self and dependents) $_____

    g)   Child support or maintenance payments
             required by prior court orders $_____

    h)   Reasonable and necessary business expenses
             for the production of income $_____

    i)   Medical expenses actually owing that are
             necessary to preserve life or health $_____

    j)   Special needs expenses for the child(ren),
             e.g., special education, therapy, etc. $_____

ACTUAL MONTHLY NET INCOME $_____

Multiply Actual Monthly Net Income by minimum statutory percentage for actual number of children of marriage:

ACTUAL NET   x 20% (one child) = $_____ *
                    x 28% (two children) = $_____
                    x 32% (three children) = $_____
                    x 40% (four children) = $_____
                    x 45% (five children) = $_____
                    x 50% (six children) = $_____

*** This is the minimum child support (usually the actual amount ordered as well)
to be paid by the noncustodial parent.**

Generic Forms

Forms are of major importance in filing a divorce. You must have the correct form for your county and Circuit Court. The first step you should take is to obtain the right forms. Use Appendix A to determine which county or Circuit Court you will need to file with. Then, either download the forms off the Circuit Court's website or go to that courthouse and get the actual forms.

These generic forms may be able to be used, depending upon the court, for those times when you cannot find the correct form or as a method to organize your information prior to going to your local courthouse. The biggest thing to remember about legal forms is that the court has absolute power to change a form, to make you fill out a new one, or to reject the form you submitted and make you redo it on the spot.

TABLE OF GENERIC FORMS

Form 1: Caption. A caption is required on the top of every form.

Form 2: Application to Proceed as a Poor Person. If your divorce goes to trial, you may want to have the court appoint an attorney to represent you. If you are unable to pay for an attorney because of a legitimate financial need, the court may be able to provide one.

Form 3: Petition for Order of Protection. In order to get court protection from a family member or from someone you had a relationship with, you will need to request that protection in a petition to the court.

Form 4: Stipulation. If you are filing for a no-fault divorce in Illinois, you and your spouse must live apart for a period of two years. This document lets both spouses agree to waive (or ignore) that two-year period.

Form 5: Joint Petition for Simplified Dissolution of Marriage. In a simplified dissolution, the petition would be the first document filed with the court in order to begin the divorce.

All forms begin with an item called a Caption. This provides the information as to the state, the Circuit Court, and the county on the first lines. Following that are the names of the parties, the court assigned number of the case, and what type of form this is.

Captions are placed at the top of the first page of the form. If a form runs more than one page, remember to number each page.

This is a generic Caption.

STATE OF ILLINOIS
IN THE CIRCUIT COURT OF THE [number of circuit] **JUDICIAL CIRCUIT**
OF [name of county] **COUNTY**

IN RE THE MARRIAGE OF:)
)
[your name]   )
)
        Petitioner   )
)
    and   )
)
[your spouse's name]   )
)
       Respondent   )

[Title of Form]

STATE OF ILLINOIS
IN THE CIRCUIT COURT OF THE _____ JUDICIAL CIRCUIT
OF _____ COUNTY

IN RE THE MARRIAGE OF:)
)
[your name]   )
)
          Petitioner   )
                           .   )   No: _____
)
     and   )
)
[your spouse's name]   )
)
          Respondent   )

APPLICATION TO PROCEED AS A POOR PERSON

I, _____, age _____, on my own behalf and under oath state:

1. I am unable to pay the costs of this proceeding.

2. My current occupation, sources of income, or public aid is: _____
_____
_____

3. My income for the preceding year was: _____

4. I expect my income for this year to be: _____

5. The names and ages people who are dependent on me for support are:
_____
_____
_____
_____
_____
_____

6. My assets are:
   Real Estate: _____
_____
_____

Personal Property: _____

_____

_____

7. I have not filed a similar application in the last year.

8. I have a meritorious claim.

Under the penalties of perjury as provided in the law Section 5/1-109 of the code of Civil Procedure, I certify that the statements in this document are true and correct, except for those matters that I have specifically stated to be on information and belief, which I believe to be true.

_____

Date Signed: _____

STATE OF ILLINOIS
IN THE CIRCUIT COURT OF THE _____ JUDICIAL CIRCUIT
OF _____ COUNTY

IN RE THE MARRIAGE OF:)
)
[your name]   )
)
        Petitioner   )
)   No: _____
        and   )
)
[your spouse's name]   )
)
        Respondent   )

PETITION FOR ORDER OF PROTECTION

TYPE OF PROTECTION SOUGHT:

        ____ EMERGENCY

        ____ INTERIM

        ____ PLENARY

PETITIONER'S INFORMATION:
NAME: _____
ADDRESS: _____
_____
DOB: ____/____/____ SOCIAL SECURITY NUMBER: _____ SEX: ____

RESPONDENT'S INFORMATION:
NAME: _____
ADDRESS: _____
_____
DOB: ____/____/____ SOCIAL SECURITY NUMBER: _____ SEX: ____
RACE: _____ HEIGHT: _____ WEIGHT: _____ HAIR: _____ EYES: _____
WORK ADDRESS: _____
_____

Is Respondent a law enforcement officer? _____

Is Respondent armed?   ____

Is Respondent dangerous? _____

Is Respondent suicidal? _____

What is relationship between Petitioner and Respondent? _____

In accordance with the Illinois Domestic Violence Act, I (Petitioner) request this Order of protection to protect ____ myself ____ minor children in my household, because:

_____

_____

_____

REMEDIES: (what I want the court to order)

_____

_____

_____

_____

_____

_____

[petitioner signature]

Date Signed: _____

STATE OF ILLINOIS
IN THE CIRCUIT COURT OF THE _____ JUDICIAL CIRCUIT
OF _____ COUNTY

IN RE THE MARRIAGE OF:)
)
[your name]   )
)
            Petitioner   )
)   No: _____
        and   )
)
[your spouse's name]   )
)
            Respondent   )

STIPULATION

NOW COME _____ and _____,
having been first duly sworn upon oath, and state that they have resided separate and apart
for a period in excess of _____ months and that the two (2) year period of continuous
separation as required by 750 ILCS 5/401 (2) is waived by each of the parties hereto.

_____
[you]

Subscribed and sworn to me on _____/_____/_____

_____
NOTARY PUBLIC

_____
[your spouse]

Subscribed and sworn to me on _____/_____/_____

_____
NOTARY PUBLIC

STATE OF ILLINOIS
IN THE CIRCUIT COURT OF THE _____ JUDICIAL CIRCUIT
OF _____ COUNTY

IN RE THE MARRIAGE OF:)
)
[your name]   )
)
      Petitioner   )
)   No: _____
      and   )
)
[your spouse's name]   )
)
      Respondent   )

JOINT PETITION FOR SIMPLIFIED DISSOLUTION OF MARRIAGE

Now comes (petitioner/plaintiff) _____, without counsel, and (respondent/defendant) _____, without counsel and hereby petitions this Honorable Court for a dissolution of the marriage between Petitioner/Plaintiff and Respondent/Defendant. In support of this petition for dissolution of marriage, the parties state as follows:

1. The Plaintiff is presently _____ years old; Plaintiff's occupation is _____; Plaintiff lives at _____, _____, Illinois; and HAS/HAS NOT (choose one) lived in the State of Illinois for at least 90-days immediately prior to the filing of this document.

2. The Defendant is presently _____ years old; Defendant's occupation is _____; Plaintiff lives at _____, _____, Illinois; and HAS/HAS NOT (choose one) lived in the State of Illinois for at least 90-days immediately prior to the filing of this document.

3. Plaintiff and Defendant have been married for less than eight years prior to the filing of this document; the marriage took place on the date _____/_____/_____; the marriage was registered in the County of _____ in the State of _____.

4. No children were born to the Plaintiff and Defendant during this marriage; the Plaintiff and Defendant adopted no children during this marriage; and to best of the wife's _____(name of wife) knowledge, she is not pregnant.

5. The parties have lived separate and apart for a continuous period that is in excess of six months. Irreconcilable differences have caused the irretrievable breakdown of their marriage. Efforts at reconciliation have failed and future attempts at reconciliation would be both impracticable and not in the best interest of the parties. The parties have signed an affidavit waiving the requirement for a continuous period living separate and apart in excess of two-years. The parties have lived separate and apart since _____/_____/_____.

6. Neither party is dependent on the other for spousal support (alimony/maintenance). Both parties acknowledge that consulting with attorneys could help determine if either is eligible for spousal support. Both parties are willing to waive the right to spousal support.

7. Neither Plaintiff nor Defendant has any interest in real estate (real property).

8. Both parties have disclosed to each other all assets owned by either party and tax returns for the years of the marriage.

9. Neither Plaintiff nor Defendant has a gross annual income in excess of $20,000. Plaintiff's gross annual income is $_____. Defendant's gross annual income is $_____. The total annual income of both parties is less than $35,000.00

10. The total fair market value of all marital property, after any deductions for liens or encumbrances, is less than $10,000. The parties have executed a written agreement dividing all assets with value greater than $100. The parties have executed a written agreement dividing responsibility for debts and financial liabilities. A copy of this agreement, signed by both parties, is attached to this document.

11. (Optional) The wife (name) _____ is known by a former/maiden name of _____; and she wishes to return to that name.

THE PARTIES REQUEST THAT THE COURT ORDER AS FOLLOWS:

A. That the parties be awarded a Judgement of Dissolution of Marriage which end the legal marriage between the parties.
B. That the written agreement of the parties that divides marital assets, debts, and liabilities (attached) is put into the final Order by the Court.
C. (Optional) That the wife be restored to her former/maiden name.
D. That this Court grant the parties any relief that may be just.

_____   _____
         [Plaintiff]   [Defendant]

DATE SIGNED: _____/_____/_____   _____/_____/_____

Sample
Agreements

This appendix provides an outline for the common items that usually appear in a Joint Parenting Agreement and a Marital Settlement Agreement. Remember, everyone is different and you may need additional clauses in such an agreement, especially in the case of special needs children and disabled adults. Your attorney is in the best position to help you create your own tailored agreement.

SAMPLE JOINT PARENTING AGREEMENT

Begin the agreement with the full names of the parties and, if you have filed in court, the case number assigned to your case.

SECTION I. GENERAL INFO

   A.   The Parties to the Divorce
   - provide the name, age and current address of each party
   - provide the date and county/state where they were married
   - provide dates separated, time living apart, date divorce filed

   B.   The Children
   - state the name, the sex, and the birth date of each child
   - state where each child has been living, the school they attend; list medical or other special needs each child requires

SECTION II. CUSTODY

   A.   Details of Custody
   - state that both parties agree to what is in the best interest of child/children
   - state where the child/children are to live
   - list how each parent is planning to make this living situation work

SECTION III. TIME WITH EACH PARENT

   A.   Weekly Schedule
   - list the time each parent has planned to spend with the child/children
   - include scheduling for when school is in session, sports, lessons, outside activities, and special activities at the school

   B.   Weekend Schedule
   - if the parents are taking turns on time with the child/children during weekends, list that schedule here

---

Example:

Father has children every other weekend from Friday night at 6 p.m. until Sunday night at 7 p.m.

   C.   Holiday Schedule
   - list holidays and important days for the parents and who will have the child/children on that day
   - if holidays change by the year, include this here

D.   Vacation Time
- if one parent has custody of the children for vacations, include that schedule here

E.   Other
- leave an opening for additional times when one parent or the other may want the children, such as a family funeral, family reunion, or any other atypical event

F.   Changing this schedule
- make provisions for parents to change this schedule. Some changes may need to be approved by the court. There should be some thought as to how to change a schedule in case of an emergency.
- make provisions for handling conflicts between the parents for scheduling problems

G.   Travel
- if certain travel with the children outside Illinois is anticipated, that schedule should be included; otherwise, the parent may need to go into court for permission

SECTION IV. CHILD SUPPORT

A.   Schedule
- list the amount of the support and when it is due
- list when child support is to begin and when it is to end

B.   Education
- list each parent's level of support for a child's education
- if a child has special educational needs, include that
- address who will pay for college, if the child will contribute, and what rights a contributing parent has (many times a parent will agree to contribute so much as long as he or she gets the right to select the college)

C.   Other
- address what will happen if the person paying support loses his/her job
- address bonuses or other additional income
- make some provision for conflicts between the parents regarding support

(Both parties will need to sign and date the agreement, which is then presented to the court for review.)

MARITAL SETTLEMENT AGREEMENT

Begin the agreement with the full names of the parties and, if you have filed in court, the case number assigned to your case.

A.   The parties to the divorce
- provide the name, age, and current address of each party
- provide the date and county/state where they were married
- provide dates separated, time living apart, date divorce filed

B.   The children
- state the name, the sex, and the birth date of each child

C.   State the grounds for the divorce

D.   Reference the Joint Parenting Agreement, requesting that under the law that agreement become part of this one

E.   Discuss the agreement on maintenance, even if there is no maintenance

F.   List all marital property and who gets each item

G.   Discuss pensions, Social Security payments, life insurance and who has rights to each pension

H.   List all debts and who now has responsibility for each

(Both parties will need to sign and date the agreement, which is then presented to the court for review.)

Index